Finding Mother

A JOURNEY OF LOSS AND LOVE

Teacher's Guide

Reading Comprehension
Character Education
Secondary Students

An Anthology of the
Finding Mother Series
of Four Chronological Memoirs

Dr. Grace LaJoy Henderson

This Teacher's Guide must be used in conjunction with the Student Workbook for Finding Mother Series of four books or Finding Mother: A Journey of Loss and Love

FINDING MOTHER – TEACHER'S GUIDE
READING COMPREHENSION AND CHARACTER EDUCATION
Copyright ©2021 Grace LaJoy Henderson
Published by Inspirations by Grace LaJoy
Raymore, MO www.gracelajoy.com

ISBN: 978-1-7341868-9-5

All rights reserved. No portion of this book may be copied, reproduced or transmitted in any form without prior written permission from the publisher.

Printed in the United States of America

"Dr. Grace LaJoy's story needs to be an integral part of every secondary school and on every library bookshelf."
~Dr. Kerry C. Dixon, Educator

"My Finding Mother Series is a memorable keepsake, something that will go down in history."
~Dr. Grace LaJoy Henderson

TABLE OF CONTENTS

A Word from the Author   Page 11

Worksheets for Book One
Finding Mother After Five Decade: A Story of Hope

Lesson One
- Main Idea and Supporting Details
- Sequencing
- Literary Techniques: Flashback
- Identifying Cause and Effect
- Point of View
- Character Trait Discussion – *Empathetic*

Lesson Two
- Main Idea and Supporting Details
- Plot Analysis: Conflict
- Identifying Cause and Effect
- Context Clues
- Interpreting and Evaluating Information
- Character Trait Discussion – *Grateful*

Lesson Three
- Main Idea and Supporting Details
- Sequencing
- Plot Analysis: Conflict
- Identifying Cause and Effect
- Interpreting and Evaluating Information
- Character Trait Discussion – *Determined*

Lesson Four
- Main Idea and Supporting Details
- Sequencing
- Text Structure: Chronological Order
- Identifying Cause and Effect
- Interpreting and Evaluating Information
- Character Trait Discussion – *Tireless*

Lesson Five
- Main Idea and Supporting Details
- Sequencing
- Identifying Cause and Effect
- Interpreting and Evaluating Information
- Story Structure and Author Intention
- Character Trait Discussion – *Hopeful*

Lesson Six
- Main Idea and Supporting Details
- Sequencing
- Plot Analysis: Rising Action
- Identifying Cause and Effect
- Interpreting and Evaluating Information
- Character Trait Discussion – *Hopelessness*

Lesson Seven
- Main Idea and Supporting Details
- Plot Analysis: Climax
- Identifying Cause and Effect
- Interpreting and Evaluating Information
- Character Trait Discussion – *Euphoric*

Worksheets for Book Two
After the Reunion: A Story of Acceptance

Lesson One
- Main Idea and Supporting Details
- Sequencing
- Plot Analysis
- Identifying Cause and Effect
- Textual Evidence
- Point of View
- Character Trait Discussion – *Zealous*

Lesson Two
- Main Idea and Supporting Details
- Sequencing
- Themes: Expectation Vs. Reality
- Literary Techniques: Emotive Language
- Identifying Cause and Effect
- Textual Evidence
- Character Trait Discussion: *Sedulous*

Lesson Three
- Main Idea and Supporting Details
- Sequencing
- Literary Technique: Descriptive Language
- Literary Elements: Mood
- Identifying Cause and Effect
- Textual Evidence
- Character Trait Discussion – *Open-minded*

Lesson Four
- Main Idea and Supporting Details
- Sequencing
- Plot Analysis: Falling Action
- Identifying Cause and Effect
- Character Transformation
- Character Trait Discussion – *Patient*

Lesson Five
- Main Idea and Supporting Details
- Plot Analysis: Resolution
- Identifying Cause and Effect
- Textual Evidence
- Author's Intention
- Story Summary
- Character Trait Discussion – *Tenaciousness*

Worksheets for Book Three
Reuniting with Mother: A Story of Tenacity

Lesson One
- Main Idea and Supporting Details
- Sequencing
- Plot Analysis
- Point of View
- Identifying Cause and Effect
- Comparing and Contrasting
- Character Analysis
- Contextual Meaning
- Character Trait Discussion – *Benevolent*

Lesson Two
- Main Idea and Supporting Details
- Sequencing
- Point of Vies
- Genre
- Author's Purpose
- Identifying Cause and Effect
- Comparing and Contrasting
- Interpreting and Evaluating Information
- Character Trait Evidence
- Contextual Meaning
- Character Trait Discussion – *Thoughtful*

Lesson Three
- Main Idea and Supporting Details
- Sequencing
- Author's Purpose
- Identifying Cause and Effect
- Interpreting and Evaluating Information
- Contextual Meaning
- Character Analysis
- Character Trait Discussion – *Altruistic*

Lesson Four
- Main Idea and Supporting Details
- Sequencing
- Author's Purpose
- Identifying Cause and Effect
- Interpreting and Evaluating Information
- Comparing and Contrasting
- Language: Idioms
- Inference
- Character Analysis
- Character Trait Discussion – *Loving*

Lesson Five
- Main Idea and Supporting Details
- Sequencing
- Author's Purpose
- Identifying Cause and Effect
- Literary Techniques: Descriptive Language
- Character Analysis
- Character Trait Discussion – *Accommodating*

Lesson Six
- Main Idea and Supporting Details
- Character Analysis: Geneva
- Identifying Cause and Effect
- Interpreting and Evaluating Information
- Contetual Meaning
- Character Trait Discussion – *Acquiescent*

Lesson Seven
- Main Idea and Supporting Details
- Literary Devices: Flashback
- Literary Elements: Tone
- Identifying Cause and Effect
- Contextual Meaning
- Inference
- Character Trait Discussion – *Affable*

Worksheets for Book Three
Reuniting with Mother: A Story of Tenacity Continued...

Lesson Eight
- Main Idea and Supporting Details
- Character Analysis
- Identifying Cause and Effect
- Interpreting and Evaluating Information
- Comparing and Contrasting
- Character Trait Discussion – *Enthusiastic*

Lesson Nine
- Main Idea and Supporting Details
- Summarizing
- Point of Vies
- Identifying Cause and Effect
- Interpreting and Evaluating Information
- Character Trait Analysis: Geneva
- Character Trait Discussion – *Appreciation*

Lesson Ten
- Main Idea and Supporting Details
- Story Elements: Dialogue
- Identifying Cause and Effect
- Reading for Information
- Contextual Meaning
- Character Trait Discussion – *Understanding*

Lesson Eleven
- Main Idea and Supporting Details
- Sequencing
- Character Analysis
- Literary Elements: Theme
- Identifying Cause and Effect
- Interpreting and Evaluating Information
- Character Trait Discussion – *Inquisitive*

Lesson Twelve
- Main Idea and Supporting Details
- Sequencing
- Literary Elements: Theme
- Figurative Language: Symbolism
- Inference
- Character Analysis
- Comparing and Contrasting
- Character Trait Discussion – *Accepting*

Worksheets for Book Four
Diary of Emotions: Thoughts and Feelings

Lesson One
- Main Idea and Supporting Details
- Plot Analysis: Internal Conflict
- Analyzing Characters and Incidents
- Identifying Cause and Effect
- Drawing Conclusions
- Character Trait Discussion – *Forgiving*

Lesson Two
- Main Idea and Supporting Details
- Point of View: Objective vs. Subjective Narrator
- Making Inferences
- Analyzing Characters and Incidents
- Identifying Cause and Effect
- Character Trait Discussion – *Understanding*

Lesson Three
- Main Idea and Supporting Details
- Literary Elements: Theme
- Character Analysis
- Identifying Cause and Effect
- Reading for Information
- Character Trait Discussion – *Acceptance*

Lesson Four
- Main Idea and Supporting Details
- Literary Elements: Theme
- Literary Techniques
- Identifying Cause and Effect
- Reading for Information
- Character Trait Discussion – *Curiosity*

Lesson Five
- Main Idea and Supporting Details
- Literary Elements: Tone
- Identifying Cause and Effect
- Interpreting and Evaluating Information
- Character Trait Discussion – *Adaptable*

Lesson Six
- Main Idea and Supporting Details
- Literary Elements: Style
- Identifying Cause and Effect
- Interpreting and Evaluating Information
- Character Trait Discussion – *Compassionate*

Lesson Seven
- Main Idea and Supporting Details
- Author's Purpose
- Identifying Cause and Effect
- Interpreting and Evaluating Information
- Character Trait Discussion – *Generous*

Lesson Eight
- Main Idea and Supporting Details
- Character Analysis
- Identifying Cause and Effect
- Interpreting and Evaluating Information
- Comparing and Contrasting
- Character Trait Discussion – *Sensible*

Lesson Nine
- Main Idea and Supporting Details
- Making Inferences
- Character Analysis
- Identifying Cause and Effect
- Character Trait Discussion – *Unprejudiced*

Lesson Ten
- Main Idea and Supporting Details
- Reading for Information
- Identifying Cause and Effect
- Character Trait Discussion – *Talented*

Worksheets for Book Four
Diary of Emotions: Thoughts and Feelings Continued...

Lesson Eleven
- Main Idea and Supporting Details
- Making Inferences
- Character Trait Discussion – *Perceptive*

Lesson Twelve
- Main Idea and Supporting Details
- Making Inferences
- Identifying Cause and Effect
- Character Decisions and Actions
- Character Trait Discussion – *Dutiful*

Lesson Thirteen
- Main Idea and Supporting Details
- Reading for Information
- Identifying Cause and Effect
- Interpreting and Evaluating Information
- Character Trait Discussion – *Magnanimous*

Lesson Fourteen
- Main Idea and Supporting Details
- Interpreting and Evaluating Information
- Character Trait Discussion – *Introspective*

Lesson Fifteen
- Main Idea and Supporting Details
- Making Inferences
- Reading for Information
- Identifying Cause and Effect
- Character Trait Discussion – *Rational*

Lesson Sixteen
- Main Idea and Supporting Details
- Character Decisions and Actions
- Character Trait Discussion – *Optimistic*

Lesson Seventeen
- Main Idea and Supporting Details
- Making Inferences
- Reading for Information
- Character Trait Discussion – *Practical*

Lesson Eighteen
- Main Idea and Supporting Details
- Making Inferences
- Character Trait Discussion – *Undecided*

Lesson Nineteen
- Main Idea and Supporting Details
- Reading for Information
- Interpreting and Inferring
- Character Trait Discussion – *Responsible*

Lesson Twenty
- Main Idea and Supporting Details
- Reading for Information
- Interpreting and Evaluating Information
- Character Trait Discussion – *Self-Reliant*

Lesson Twenty-One
- Main Idea and Supporting Details
- Character Decisions and Actions
- Identifying Cause and Effect
- Character Trait Discussion – *Thoughtful*

Lesson Twenty-Two
- Main Idea and Supporting Details
- Making Predictions
- Character Trait Discussion – *Capable*

Lesson Twenty-Three
- Main Idea and Supporting Details
- Making Predictions
- Identifying Cause and Effect
- Character Trait Discussion – *Giving*

Worksheets for Book Four
Diary of Emotions: Thoughts and Feelings Continued...

Lesson Twenty-Four
- Main Idea and Supporting Details
- Identifying Cause and Effect
- Character Trait Discussion – *Initiator*

Lesson Twenty-Five
- Main Idea and Supporting Details
- Interpreting and Evaluating Information
- Character Trait Discussion – *Complaisant*

Lesson Twenty-Six
- Main Idea and Supporting Details
- Textual Evidence
- Character Trait Discussion – *Respectfulness*

Lesson Twenty-Seven
- Main Idea and Supporting Details
- Analyzing Character
- Making Inferences and Drawing Conclusions
- Character Trait Discussion – *Appreciative*

Lesson Twenty-Eight
- Main Idea and Supporting Details
- Making Inferences and Drawing Conclusions
- Identifying Cause and Effect
- Character Trait Discussion – *Considerate*

Lesson Twenty-Nine
- Main Idea and Supporting Details
- Reading for Information
- Analyzing Dialogue
- Identifying Cause and Effect
- Character Trait Discussion – *Supportive*

Lesson Thirty
- Main Idea and Supporting Details
- Reading for Information
- Character Decisions and Actions
- Interpreting and Evaluating Information
- Character Trait Discussion – *Charitable*

A Word from the Author

Hello, my name is Dr. Grace LaJoy Henderson, author of over 35 books.

Studies have shown when young people go through challenging situations, they often lack the skills of how to use their stories in a way that empower themselves and others. They can't see into the future to see how their life will turn out.

But, with my Finding Mother Series, they get a glimpse of what life can look like after going through various life circumstances. They will realize that it is the exact circumstance, that they are going through at this very moment, that is giving them the lemons they need to make lemonade.

They will also learn that they are not alone in many of the natural emotions, thoughts and feelings they experience. Not to mention, that some of our children may share my *exact* situation of living without their mother in their lives.

At only two years old, my mother left my siblings and I with our father whose unviability led me down a path where I experienced numerous challenges from living in foster care to becoming a teen mom.

When I wrote my foster care story, A Gifted Child in Foster Care: A Story of Resilience in 2009, I had no idea I would ever find my mother. She had been gone for 41 years when I wrote the story, so finding her seemed to be only a dream that would never, ever come true. Later, when I knew she would be around 80 years old, I gave up all hope of ever finding her alive.

But, on March 2, 2018, I found my mother after 49 years!

And I share the entire story in my Finding Mother Series.

After I completed the Finding Mother Series, I received feedback from readers. It turned out there were a lot of people who were inspired because they, too, had been trying to find a long-lost loved one with no success. My story gave them hope.

When I was growing up, with all of the other feelings that went along with my circumstances, I had no idea my story would have a positive effect on so many people. When the Sherriff removed me from a house, where my father left me and my siblings, with no food or utilities, I had no idea I would one day be writing my foster care story. When I wrote my finding mother story, I had no idea I would end up creating the Anthology, let alone creating matching workbooks, to enhance reading comprehension and character education for middle and high school students.

Our students represent the youngest branch of society but that doesn't mean they don't experience life-changing challenges. That's where my story comes in. When students experience my story, they will know that their lives, regardless of their circumstances, can be a blessing to others.

My story reveals how a foster child becomes an author and finds her mother after 49 years of separation. My finding mother series teaches students that they have the power to overcome any challenge in life; and that their challenges can be used to benefit others. Put this book in the hands of your students and watch them put my theories of self-development into practice as they realize the power of their own stories.

Book 1

Finding Mother

Answer Keys
Chapters 1-7

Lesson One - Answers

> This lesson coincides with Chapter 1 of the book, 'Finding Mother'. The purpose of this lesson is to analyze the reason for the main character's problem using key points from the text.
> **Chapter One – "Before Mother Left"**

Main Idea and Supporting Details

Place an X on the line beside the main idea of the text.

_____ The author's father physically harmed her mother.

_____**X**_____ **The author's mother was mentally unfit to care for her family.**

_____ The author empathized with her father because he cared for her.

The <u>four</u> statements below "support" the main idea. Fill in the blanks with the correct word.

(a) Mother would often experience **episodes**, which resulted in the harming of the author and her siblings. (Page 16)

(b) Jerome told the author that their **father** is not to be blamed for their mother's condition. (Page 16)

(c) Father experienced a lot of **stress** and **disappointment** due to his wife having a mental illness. (Page 17)

(d) Father did not receive the **support** he desired from his wife. (Page 17)

Sequencing

Rearrange the following lines from Chapter 1 by numbering them correctly.

(4) The author blamed her father for her mother's emotional state. (Page 16)

(2) The author has some very heartbreaking memories of her mother. (Page 15)

(6) Father was disappointed due to his wife having a mental illness. (Page 17)

(1) Mother left when the author was only two years old. (Page 15)

(3) Father had called the authorities to take mother to a mental hospital. (Page 15)

(5) The author remembers her mother beating her with a broomstick once. (Page 17)

Literary Techniques: Flashback

Using flashbacks as a story device, the author takes readers back in time to explain something that happened. Answer the following questions in a word or more.

(a) Which year or decade is the author recalling events from?   **1969** (Page 15)

(b) How old was the author during that time?   **two years old** (Page 15)

Identifying Cause and Effect

"I heard stories about my mother's mental illness causing her to experience episodes, which resulted in her harming my siblings and me."

What is the Cause? my mother's mental illness

What is the Effect? Episodes, which resulted her harming my siblings and me.

Point of View

'Point of view' means the position from which something or someone is observed.

'First Person' is when the story is told from the point of view of a character.   *E.g. I, we, me, us*

'Second Person' is when the narrator talks to the reader.   *E.g. you, yours*

'Third Person' is when the narrator is not a part of the story.   *E.g. he, she, it*

(a) Who is telling the story in Chapter 1?   **The author / protagonist**

(b) Circle the narrator's point of view in Chapter 1: (**First**) Second, Third

Character Trait Discussion

The character trait for Chapter 1 is "empathetic".

Empathetic means showing the ability to understand and share the feelings of another.

Read the statement below. Then choose one of the questions below and answer it. Write your answer in the space provided then discuss it with your group.

The author has expressed sorrow for her mother's predicament in the story. She even says that her mother did not deserve any abuse from her father.

1. Would you feel empathy if someone you loved was treated badly? Explain why or why not.

2. Describe a situation where you felt empathetic towards someone or something.

3. Do you think it is important to show empathy to those who are going through something difficult? Explain and include an example if possible.

_____Answers will vary from learner to learner._____

Lesson Two – Answers

This lesson coincides with Chapter 2 of the book, 'Finding Mother'. The purpose of this lesson is to analyze the feelings of the main character after a specific event.
Chapter Two – "After Mother Left"

Main Idea and Supporting Details

Place an "X" on the line beside the main idea of Chapter 2.

_____X_____ The author misses her mother and wants to find her.

_____ The author feels bad about her own mother not wanting to receive her.

_____ The author's father is sensible and genuinely cares about his family.

The four statements below "support" the main idea. Fill in the blanks with the correct word.

(a) The protagonist did not **agree** with what her father said about her mother. (Page 19)

(b) The protagonist felt that her grandmother and father were just making excuses because they **resented** her mother. (Page 20)

(c) The protagonist felt **afraid** to tell her father that she wanted to find her mother. (Page 22)

(d) Wanting to know her mother's side of the story, **motivated** the author to find her. (Page 22)

Plot Analysis: Conflict

The conflict in a story is the struggle faced by two opposing forces. It is usually the main character that faces some sort of conflict, either with another character (person vs. person) or with themselves (person vs. self).

In 'Finding Mother', the author does not believe her father's reasons for her mother leaving and rejecting her. Although she misses her mother terribly, the author is hesitant to tell her father that she wants to find her.
What kind of conflict do you think the author is facing here? Circle the letter for the correct answer.

a) Person vs. Person   b) Person vs. Self   **c) Both**

17

Identifying Cause and Effect

"My father often complained about how my mother got a job working for a dry cleaner and was terminated when she refused to do things according to her boss's instructions."

What is the cause? <u>Mother refused to do things according to her boss's instructions.</u>

What is the effect? <u>She was terminated from the job.</u>

Note to teacher: The cause could also be that mother was terminated from her job, with the effect being father often complained.

Context Clues

Read the following line from the story, and figure out the meaning of the highlighted word using clues in the sentence. Circle the letter for the correct answer once you are sure.

He **mocked** her voice as he reminisced about the way she used to say, "One of these days I'm going to go far, far away."

a) insulted

b) made fun of

c) imitated

Interpreting and Evaluating Information

How does the author truly feel about the things her father said about her mother? Write three things from Chapter 2.

1. <u>She did not like or agree with most of what he said about her mother.</u> (Page 19)

2. <u>She felt that he was the reason for her leaving.</u> (Page 19)

3. <u>She felt that he was just making up excuses.</u> (Page 19)

Character Trait Discussion

The character trait for Chapter 2 is "grateful".

Grateful means feeling or showing an appreciation for something done or received.

Read the statement below. Then choose one of the questions below and answer it. Write your answer in the space provided then discuss it with your group.

In the story, the author said she felt grateful that her mother left to get the break she needed.

1. Name one or more things a person may do when they are feeling grateful. Provide one or more examples for each thing you name.

2. What is something that you are extremely grateful for right now?

3. How would you teach someone to be grateful?

_____**Answers will vary from learner to learner.**_____

_____

_____

_____

_____

_____

_____

_____

_____

_____

_____

Lesson Three - Answers

This lesson coincides with Chapter 3 of the book, 'Finding Mother'. The purpose of this lesson is to understand the difficulties faced by the main character in achieving her goal.
Chapter Three – "The Search"

Main Idea and Supporting Details

Place an "X" on the line beside the main idea of the text.

_____ Grace uses many online and offline resources to locate her mother.

_____ Grace is hoping that her mother will respond to her letters.

_____X_____ **Grace keeps trying hard to find her mother though her efforts are in vain.**

The four statements below "support" the main idea. Fill in the blanks with the correct word.

(a) Grace wanted to find her mother even though she was afraid of being **rejected**. (Page 23)

(b) Grace requested for the marriage license and application for her parents from the **State Department of Public Health**. (Page 25)

(c) Grace could not wait to search for her mother using her **social security number** and her **last name**. (Page 27)

(d) Grace sent a letter to four women named **Geneva**, hoping that one of them would be her mother. (Page 28)

Sequencing

Following the timeline of Grace's search techniques in Chapter 3, rearrange the following events in the correct order.

(4) She then used online white pages to search for addresses and phone numbers. (Page 26)

(3) She later visited a couple of Genealogical Research Libraries. (Page 25)

(1) Grace went to the local Social Security Administration office to ask them for help. (Page 24)

(5) Then she contacted an online people locator service. (Page 26)

(6) Finally, she sent out a letter to four women who shared her mother's name. (Page 28)

(2) She asked for her parents' marriage license from the State Dept. of Public Health. (Page 25)

Plot Analysis: Conflict

The central conflict is the main problem in a story. The conflict makes a story interesting to read and shows the motivations of the characters, as well as the consequences of their actions. Chapter 1 and 2 of 'Finding Mother' introduced us to Grace's family with some background information. What is the main conflict for Grace in Chapter 3?

Sample answer: <u>The main conflict for Grace in chapter 3 is not being able to find her mother. She uses many techniques and resources to search for her mother with the help of the information she has. However, no matter what she tries, there is no evidence or trace of her mother's whereabouts.</u>

Identifying Cause and Effect

"I was disappointed in her as I felt like she did not care what happened to the twin boys."

What is the cause? <u>I felt like she did not care what happened to the twin boys.</u>

What is the effect? <u>I was disappointed in her.</u>

Interpreting and Evaluating Information

Why did the excitement of finding her mother start to dwindle for Grace?
Circle the letter for the correct answer.

a) None of her search attempts was successful. (Page 28)

b) The Calvin she spoke to was not the one she was looking for. (Page 27)

c) None of the four women she wrote to was her mother. (Page 28)

d) All of the above.

Character Trait Discussion

The character trait for Chapter 3 is "determined".

Determined means having made a firm decision and being resolved not to change it.

Read the statement below. Then choose one of the questions below and answer it. Write your answer in the space provided then discuss it with your group.

In Chapter 3, we see how determined Grace is to find her mother through all her search attempts and techniques.

1. Describe a time when you felt determined to achieve something?

2. Do you know someone who has great determination in life? If so, who? What has this person done to show that they have determination?

3. Why do you think that it is good to be determined? Name at least one advantage or disadvantage to being determined?

_____**Answers will vary from learner to learner.**_____

_____

_____

_____

_____

_____

_____

_____

_____

_____

_____

Lesson Four - Answers

This lesson coincides with Chapter 4 of the book, 'Finding Mother'. The purpose of this lesson is to analyze some information that adds more significance to the plot.
Chapter Four – "The Search Continues"

Main Idea and Supporting Details

Place an "X" on the line beside the main idea of the text.

_____ Grace is still unable to find her mother despite several searches.

_____X_____ **Grace discovers some new information about her birth and her mother.**

_____ Grace's brother had kept their parents' divorce order for many years.

The <u>four</u> statements below "support" the main idea. Fill in the blanks with the correct word.

(a) Grace's birth records showed that her **father** took her home from the hospital. (Page 32)

(b) Grace wondered if **Kevin** could be her sibling. (Page 33)

(c) Geneva's birth certificate listed Grace's **grandmother** as her birth mother. (Page 35)

(d) Geneva's original name was **Ginny**. (Page 35)

Sequencing

Say whether the following statements are true or false. Write "T" for true and "F" for false.

(a) Grace's mother had left her in Kansas City. (Page 31)   T

(b) The "state hospital" mentioned in Grace's birth records was a normal hospital. (Page 32)   F

(c) Kevin was born in the 1930s. (Page 33)   F

(d) Joe was Geneva's actual birth father. (Pages 35)   F

(e) Grace did not know that her brother had their parents' divorce order. (Page 36)   T

(f) Grace was five years old when her parents divorced. (Page 37)   T

Text Structure: Chronological Order

Authors sometimes write stories using the chronological order structure. In the chronological structure, the events in the story are told in the order they happened. It is also called "time order."

In chapter 4, the author takes us through her journey of searching for her mother by using dates to mark what happened.

Write one-line answers to say what happened in the story on the following dates.

(a) January 10, 1998 – <u>Grace sent an inquiry letter to the Superior Court, Records Information Center, requesting public information about her mother. (Page 31)</u>

(b) May 4, 1998 – <u>She received a copy of her mother's birth certificate from the State Department of Health. (Page 35)</u>

(c) September 11, 2008 – <u>Her brother gave her a copy of their father and mother's divorce order dated 1971. (Page 36)</u>

Identifying Cause and Effect

"I presumed that she did not necessarily "leave" those children in the hospital, but was unable to take them home due to being in a mental hospital at the time of their births, causing the babies to become automatic wards of the state."

What is the cause? <u>due to being in a mental hospital at the time of their births</u>

What is the effect? <u>was unable to take them home - causing the babies to become automatic wards of the state.</u>

Interpreting and Evaluating Information

Do you think Grace became more appreciative of her father at the end of the chapter?

Circle the letter for the correct answer.

a) No, she still thinks her father is responsible for her mother leaving.

b) Yes, because she felt like her father truly wanted her and it gave her security. (Page 37)

c) No, although she is ambivalent about both her parents.

Character Trait Discussion

The character trait for Chapter 4 is "tireless".

Tireless means having or showing great effort or energy.

Read the statement below. Then choose one of the questions below and answer it. Write your answer in the space provided then discuss it with your group.

In Chapter 4, Grace shows how tireless she is in continuing to search for her mother. Only after many attempts does she give up to take a break.

1. Do you think that Grace should have just given up the search for her mother at that point? Explain why or why not.

2. What is something that you would work tirelessly for?

3. Write about a time when you did not give up? What was the result?

_____**Answers will vary from learner to learner.**_____

_____

_____

_____

_____

_____

_____

_____

_____

_____

_____

_____

Lesson Five - Answers

This lesson coincides with Chapter 5 of the book, 'Finding Mother'. The purpose of this lesson is to understand the main character's motivation behind pursuing her goal.
Chapter Five – "The Search Continues"

Main Idea and Supporting Details
Place an "X" on the line beside the main idea of the text.

_____X_____ Grace is hopeful about finding her mother even though it's been forty-one years.

_____ Some kind-hearted people have come forward to help Grace find her mother.

_____ Grace has already tried to find her mother using her social security number.

The four statements below "support" the main idea. Fill in the blanks with the correct word.

(a) Grace walked into a **Private Investigator's** office to help her find her mother. (Page 39)

(b) Grace decided to use the **press release** for her new book to try to locate her mother. (Page 40)

(c) When she published her foster care story, Grace purposely included the names of her **siblings** and **mother**. (Page 42)

(d) Grace sent a **note** with **pictures** to her mother through the Social Security Administration Office. (Page 42)

Sequencing
"X" all the things that Grace did in Chapter 5 to search for her mother.

Grace searched for Geneva's biological family. (Page 39)	(X)
She paid Sherry to help her find Geneva. (Page 40)	( )
She decided to use the announcement for her new book to try locating her mother. (Page 40)	(X)
Using the address the woman found for her, Grace visited the property.	( )
She included the real names of her family in her foster care story hoping that someone would recognize it. (Page 42)	(X)
Grace went on the TV show even though they couldn't find her mother.	( )

Identifying Cause and Effect

"However, due to Joe having such a common first and last name, there were tons of them listed in the census records. As a result, it was impossible to tell which one of them was the correct one."

What is the cause? <u>due to Joe having such a common first and last name</u>

What is the effect? <u>it was impossible to tell which one of them was the correct one.</u>

Interpreting and Evaluating Information

How did Grace feel when some people volunteered to help her find her mother?

Circle the letter for the correct answer.

a) She felt that they would not be successful, but was willing to give them a chance. (Page 40)

b) She did not feel confident that they would come up with anything.

c) She was certain that they would be able to find her mother using her social security number.

Story Structure and Author Intention

Writers structure stories in different ways, depending on their reasons for writing them.

A **milieu** story structure focuses on the world surrounding the characters you create.

A **character** story structure is all about the character's growth, transformation or downfall.

An **event** story structure is about fixing an external problem where something is wrong and the characters need to set it right.

What structure is the author following for 'Finding Mother'?

Circle the letter for the correct answer.

(a) milieu　　　　(b) character　　　　**(c) event**

Character Trait Discussion

The character trait for Chapter 4 is "hopeful".
Hopeful means feeling or inspiring optimism about a future event.

Read the statement below. Then choose <u>one</u> of the questions below and answer it. Write your answer in the space provided then discuss it with your group.

In this chapter, Grace tries to remain hopeful about finding her mother one day despite several unsuccessful attempts to locate her.

1. Do you think it is good to be hopeful for things? Explain why or why not.

2. What is something you have been hopeful for something? Did you receive what you were hoping for?

3. What do you think is the right way to handle disappointment?

_____**Answers will vary from learner to learner.**_____

_____

_____

_____

_____

_____

_____

_____

_____

_____

_____

_____

Lesson Six - Answers

This lesson coincides with Chapter 6 of the book, 'Finding Mother'. The purpose of this lesson is to understand the impact of failure on the main character and how she deals with it.
Chapter Six – "Losing Hope, Then Finding a Glimmer"

Main Idea and Supporting Details

Place an "X" on the line beside the main idea of the text.

_____ Grace feels like nobody can help her find her mother.

_____X_____ Grace has almost given up hope on finding her mother.

_____ Grace imagined miraculously finding her mother though hope was dim.

The <u>four</u> statements below "support" the main idea. Fill in the blanks with the correct word.

(a) Grace felt **insignificant** when the talk shows she wrote to did not respond to her messages. (Page 45)

(b) Instead of feeling **hopeful**, she was beginning to feel **resentful**. (Page 46)

(c) Grace decided that if she could not find her mother, she would try to locate her **family** **members**. (Page 46)

(d) Grace felt good that she found **cousins** related to her mother in some way. (Page 46)

Sequencing
Write YES or NO as the answer for each statement.

(a) Grace lost hope in finding her mother during her inactive searching time.   **YES** (Page 45)

(b) She felt annoyed when the suggestions people gave her didn't work out.   **YES** (Page 45)

(c) Grace never enjoyed watching TV talk show reunions.   **NO** (Page 45)

(d) She felt happy for the people who had found their relatives even though she hadn't found hers.   **NO** (Page 46)

(e) Grace decided to watch the reunion show immediately after her friend told her about it.   **NO** (Page 47)

(f) Grace's big sister Carla had been missing for over ten years.   **YES** (Page 50)

Plot Analysis: Rising Action

The rising action in a story moves the plot closer to the climax. It is the part where obstacles stand in the way of the author achieving his/her goal.

What obstacle do you think Grace has to get through in order to achieve her goal of finding her mother?

(a) Facing the reality of perhaps never finding her at all.

(b) Dealing with endless searches, which could take years to produce any strong leads.

(c) Not being able to find a single clue about her mother's whereabouts.

(d) All of the above.

Identifying Cause and Effect

"Because of my increasingly raw feelings, I eventually stopped watching reunion shows altogether. I purposely avoided those types of shows because they revealed the harsh reality that my mother was missing and I may never find her."

What is the cause? <u>Because of my increasingly raw feelings,</u>
What is the effect? <u>I eventually stopped watching reunion shows altogether.</u>
-or-
What is the cause? <u>they revealed the harsh reality that my mother was missing and I may never find her.</u>
What is the effect? <u>I eventually stopped watching reunion shows altogether.</u>

Interpreting and Evaluating Information

Circle the letter for the correct answer.

From the feelings expressed by the author in this chapter, we can conclude that….

a) She feels frustrated and hopeless about ever finding her mother.

b) She is jealous of the people or talk show reunions because they could find their relatives.

c) She has not completely given up as she has decided to look for her siblings and mother's relatives.

(d) All of the above.

Character Trait Discussion

The character trait for Chapter 4 is "hopelessness".
Hopelessness means a feeling or state of despair.

Read the statement below. Then choose <u>one</u> of the questions below and answer it.
Write your answer in the space provided then discuss it with your group.

In this chapter, Grace is beginning to feel completely hopeless and has started feeling jealous of people who have found their long-lost family members.

1. When would you give up if you were searching for a missing relative?
2. Discuss a time when you completely lost hope in something?
3. How would you encourage someone who has lost hope in something they wanted so badly?

_____Answers will vary from learner to learner._____

_____

_____

_____

_____

Lesson Seven - Answers

This lesson coincides with Chapter 7 of the book, 'Finding Mother'. The purpose of this lesson is to analyze the techniques used by the main character to achieve her goal.
Chapter Seven – "I Found My Mother!"

Main Idea and Supporting Details

Place an "X" on the line beside the main idea of the text.

_____ Grace was about to cease searching for her mother after one last attempt.

_____ Grace could not believe that she was able to talk to her mother.

_____X_____ Grace is overjoyed about finding her mother after almost 50 years.

The four statements below "support" the main idea. Fill in the blanks with the correct word.

(a) Grace's mother Geneva, was residing at a **boarding home**. (Page 52)

(b) A woman named **April** helped Grace to connect with her mother. (Page 53)

(c) Grace felt **puzzled** about why Geneva asked her who she was after answering all of her questions. (Page 54)

(d) Grace immediately informed her brother **Jerome** about finding their mother. (Page 52)

Plot Analysis: Climax

The climax is the highest point of interest in a story. This is where the conflict is at the highest point of tension.

It was an anxious moment for Grace when she was trying to confirm if she had actually found her mother. She feels nervous while talking to Geneva on the phone hoping that she was indeed her long-lost mother.

Describe how this part of the story made you feel before and after Grace spoke to Geneva.

_____ **Expected answers:** excited, happy, anxious, eager, curious, emotional, tense _____

_____

_____

_____

Identifying Cause and Effect

"I explained to her that she was in a different state and I was in Missouri, so I could not just come right over. But, that I would come as soon as I possibly could."

What is the Cause? <u>she was in a different state and I was in Missouri</u>

What is the Effect? <u>so I could not just come right over.</u>

Interpreting and Evaluating Information
Circle the letter for correct answer for the two questions below.

What information did Grace use to finally locate her mother?
a) her name and date of birth

b) her name, date of birth and state

c) her name and social security number

Apart from this information, what prediction about her mother did Grace get right?

a) Her mother was immobile and lying in bed in a mental hospital.

b) Her mother could not remember her or her siblings.

c) Her mother was eighty-something years old.

Character Trait Discussion
The character trait for Chapter 4 is "euphoric".
Euphoric means feeling intense excitement and happiness.

Read the statement below. Then choose <u>one</u> of the questions below and answer it. Write your answer in the space provided then discuss it with your group.

In Chapter 7, Grace has finally accomplished finding her mother after 50 years, and she feels euphoric about it.

1. Write about an incident that made you feel euphoric about something.

2. How would you feel if your friend received a reward and you did not?

3. Give some examples of situations where one should feel euphoric.

_____**Answers will vary from learner to learner.**_____

_____

Book 2

Reuniting with Mother

Answer Keys
Chapters 1-5

Lesson One – Answers

> This lesson coincides with Chapter 1 of the book, 'Reuniting with Mother'. The purpose of this lesson is to understand the emotions of the characters in the story, because of an important event.
> **Chapter One – "After Finding Mother"**

Main Idea and Supporting Details

Place an X on the line beside the main idea of the text.

_____ Grace and her brothers were not sure if their mother would receive them.

_____ Grace's brothers did not want her to drive to her mother's destination.

_____X_____ **Grace was eager to see her mother as soon as possible.**

The four statements below "support" the main idea. Fill in the blanks with the correct word.

(a) Grace had waited **forty-nine** years to see her mother and could not wait any longer. (Page 69)

(b) Terrance warned Grace of a **winter storm warning** in the area where their mother lives. (Page 65)

(c) Grace's **daughter** paid for all her expenses so that she could travel to see her mother. (Page 66)

(d) Jerome suggested that they leave on **March 8th** and return on **March 11th**. (Page 66)

Sequencing

Rearrange the following lines from Chapter 1 by numbering them correctly.

(4) The following morning, Grace drove to Terrence's house to go to the airport with him. (67)

(3) Grace receives an email from the private investigator she contacted a few days ago. (66)

(6) After landing, they ate some food and boarded the connecting flight to their mother. (68)

(2) The next morning, Jerome suggested the dates when they could leave and return. (66)

(1) Grace informed Terrence, and Jerome informed Grayson about their mother. (65)

(5) They then boarded the flight departing from Kansas City to a connecting flight. (67)

Plot Analysis: Exposition

The exposition is the beginning of the story where the characters and setting are introduced. Complete the box below with details of the exposition in Chapter 1.

Exposition

a. Setting: **Kansas City**

b. Time: **March, Winter**

c. Main character's name: **Grace**

d. Secondary characters: **Jerome, Terrence, Grayson**

e. Mood: **anxious, tense, anticipating**

f. Point of view: **First Person**

Identifying Cause and Effect

"Excited about me finally finding my mother, my daughter paid all my expenses to reunite with her, which included my plane ticket."

What is the cause? <u>Excited about me finally finding my mother.</u>

What is the Effect? <u>my daughter paid all my expenses to reunite with her, which included my plane ticket.</u>

Textual Evidence

Cite two lines from the text to show that Grace was nervous about visiting her mother. Explain why you picked those lines in the second box.

Textual Evidence	Explanation
1. I stated, "I am very tired and anxious, yet nervous." 2. I said a short prayer hoping that everything would go well and that our mother would receive us.	These two lines from the text show that Grace feels anxious about seeing her mother after a very long time. She even says a prayer hoping that her mother would receive them. She was afraid about her father's warning being true.

Character Trait Discussion

The character trait for Chapter 1 is "zealous".
Zealous means showing great enthusiasm for a cause or objective.

Read the statement below. Then choose one of the questions below and answer it. Write your answer in the space provided then discuss it with your group.

In this chapter, Graces says that she feels zealous about finally getting to see her mother again.

1. Would you feel zealous about meeting a long lost relative after many years? What would you do when you finally meet them?

2. What are some things that would make you zealous?

3. Do you think it is good to be zealous? Why or why not?

_____**Answers will vary from learner to learner.** _____

Lesson Two - Answers

> This lesson coincides with Chapter 2 of the book, 'Reuniting with Mother'. The purpose of this lesson is to understand the negative feelings of the characters after an unexpected outcome.
> **Chapter Two – "Seeing Mother After 49 Years"**

Main Idea and Supporting Details
Place an X on the line beside the main idea of the text.

_____ Grace and her brothers traveled far to see their mother.

____**X**_____ **Grace and her brothers felt disappointed that their mother didn't accept them.**

_____ Geneva did not appear the way Grace imagined her to be.

The four statements below "support" the main idea. Fill in the blanks with the correct word.

(a) Grace felt **unsure** if the woman they were visiting was actually her mother. (Page 72)

(b) When Geneva did not believe they were her children, Grace told her that she had brought her **birth certificate**. (Page 72)

(c) Grace and her brothers pleading with Geneva to accept them seemed **useless**. (Page 73)

(d) Ashley reminded them that Geneva had a mental **illness** and may need time to accept them. (Page 74)

Sequencing
Circle the letter for the correct answer based on the events in Chapter 2.

1. What did Grace think when she first looked at Geneva?
   a. She decided that she wasn't her mother right away.
   b. It triggered memories of how she desired to take care of her. (Page 71)
   c. She did not doubt that the woman was her mother because she felt excited.

2. Did Geneva look anything like how Grace expected her to be?
   a. No. Grace was surprised that Geneva did not look like her and was not tall. (Page 71)
   b. Yes. Geneva looked like her youthful self in the pictures, but aged now.
   c. No. Geneva did not look like she would be related to them at all.

3. Did Geneva accept the gift that Grace had brought for her?
   a. Although tempted to accept it at first, she refused it. (Page 73)
   b. Yes, she was very interested in the gift and accepted it.
   c. No, she refused it before Grace even took it out of her bag.

Themes: Expectation Vs. Reality

The theme is the main idea or underlying message in a literary work, which may be stated directly or indirectly. One of the themes in this chapter is "expectation vs. reality".

Grace has certain expectations about the time she would meet her mother. However, the outcome of the event turned out to be different.

Complete the table below based on what Grace expected to happen versus what actually happened when she met her mother.

Expectations	Reality
Grace had a picture in her mind of Geneva based on a young adult picture of her in her twenties.	Geneva did not look anything like the woman in the picture.
The woman in the picture was well-dressed, with styled hair, a round face with a smooth complexion, light colored skin, slightly slanted eyes, full lips and white teeth with a bright, beautiful smile.	Geneva had frizzy grey hair, her face was oval-shaped with a weary look in her eyes and only a few teeth left.
Grace thought that Geneva would look like her and even be tall.	Geneva did not look like Grace, neither was she tall.
Grace expected her father's warning about Geneva rejecting them to be untrue.	Her father's warning about Geneva turned out to be true.
Grace expected to meet April when they arrived at the boarding house.	Grace and her brother met a woman named Ashley instead.

Literary Techniques: Emotive Language

Emotive language is a literary device that writers employ in order to stir the reader's emotions. They may intentionally use certain emotional words to kindle feelings of empathy, sadness or joy in the reader.

Pick words from Chapter 2 that the writer has used for the following:

Sadness: **disappointing** **heartbroken** **distraught** **devastating**
            (Page 73)   (Page 73)   (Page 75)   (Page 76)

Identifying Cause and Effect

"The way Geneva looked each of us in the face and rejected us without any remorse. I absolutely did not like the woman who we had just encountered, and I did not want her as my mother."

What is the Cause? <u>Geneva looked at each of us in the face and rejected us without any remorse.</u>

What is the Effect? <u>I absolutely did not like the woman who we had just encountered, and I did not want her as my mother.</u>

Textual Evidence

Cite <u>two</u> examples from the text to show that Geneva was uncomfortable and suspicious about her visitors.

Textual Evidence	Textual Evidence
1. She seemed afraid and overwhelmed by all of our questions.	2. She looked up at my three big and tall brothers, then glared at me and said, "I don't know who you are. I'm not going to talk to anybody because I don't know you all."

Character Trait Discussion

The character trait for Chapter 1 is "sedulous".
Sedulous means careful and using a lot of effort.

Read the statement below. Then choose <u>one</u> of the questions below and answer it. Write your answer in the space provided then discuss it with your group.

In this chapter, we see how sedulous Grace is about visiting Geneva, despite the risk of meeting the wrong woman. She has always put in a lot of effort for this cause and finally accomplished it.

1. Would you remain sedulous even if what you are trying to achieve will take years to accomplish? Why or why not?

2. Describe something that you would work sedulously for and state your reasons.

3. Do you know someone who is sedulous about something? Describe them and their cause.

Answers will vary from learner to learner.

Lesson Three - Answers

> This lesson coincides with Chapter 3 of the book, 'Reuniting with Mother'. The purpose of this lesson is to analyze clues and key information in the text to interpret the outcome of the main event.
> **Chapter Three – "Will Mother Accept Us?"**

Main Idea and Supporting Details
Place an X on the line beside the main idea of the text.

_____X_____ Grace was determined to get Geneva to warm up to her and her brothers.

_____ Grace coaxed Geneva into talking by buying some of her favorite things.

_____ Geneva honestly did not recognize Grace and her brothers.

The four statements below "support" the main idea. Fill in the blanks with the correct word.

(a) Miss Davis told Grace that if she brought Geneva **cigarettes**, she would sit

with her and talk. (Page 80)

(b) Geneva got off the bus and **limped** across the street towards the boarding home. (Page 81)

(c) Grace handed Geneva a list of **phone numbers** that Jerome had made for her. (Page 83)

(d) She also gave Geneva a copy of her own **birth certificate**. (Page 83)

Sequencing
Look at the following events from Chapter 3 and number the boxes according to the order in which they happened.

4 After the blue bus arrived, Geneva got off and started walking to the boarding house.

1 Miss Davis directed Grace to the corner store where she could buy the things for Geneva.

5 Once inside Geneva's room, Grace handed her the items she had bought, list of contact details that Jerome made and showed her some pictures of her family.

3 Grace and her brothers waited anxiously for the blue bus to arrive with Geneva.

2 Grace and her brother bought cigarettes, coffee, shampoo, lotion, deodorant and a bar of soap for Geneva.

Literary Techniques: Descriptive Language

Through descriptive language, the author informs readers about what a person, place, object or situation is like.

How does Grace describe Geneva's room in chapter 3? (Page 80)

Furniture: **three beds, four-drawer dresser, two nightstands, one closet**

Decoration: **large piece of framed artwork hanging on the wall**

Colors: **light color paint on the walls**

Tidiness: **bed covers looked clean, floor was shining, no clutter**

Literary Elements: Mood

Moods in literature not only describe how a person feels, but also the atmosphere of groups of people, places, time periods, events, etc.

Based on your analysis of Chapter 3, how is the mood at the beginning of the chapter and at the end?

Beginning	End
The mood at the beginning of the chapter was intense as it heightens the anticipation of the reader. This is because we want to know if Geneva would accept Grace and her siblings.	There is a sense of relief and calm at the end of the chapter as Geneva finally begins to warm up to Grace after seeing the photos and birth certificates.

Identifying Cause and Effect

"I felt amazed because this was the first sign of her showing that she actually knew who we were! This made me feel a little more confident that this woman was indeed my mother."

What is the Cause? <u>...this was the first sign of her showing that she actually knew who we were!</u>

What is the Effect? <u>This made me feel a little more confident that this woman was indeed my mother.</u>

Textual Evidence

Cite two examples from the text to show that Geneva cared for Grace and her siblings.

Textual Evidence	Explanation
1. The look on her face told me she was not happy to hear that, and I detected that she was experiencing some mixed feelings.	1. Grace could tell by Geneva's facial expressions that she felt bad that their father left them alone after she had left
2. Then, I mentioned to her that we did not know where Carla was. She seemed genuinely concerned about Carla missing. She said, "That's weird that nobody knows where she is!"	2. Even though Geneva had not opened up completely, she seemed surprised that Carla was missing and nobody knew where she was.

Character Trait Discussion
The character trait for Chapter 3 is "open-minded".
Open-minded means you are willing to consider new ideas without prejudice.

Read the statement below. Then choose <u>one</u> of the questions below and answer it. Write your answer in the space provided then discuss it with your group.

Grace has been open-minded ever since she began the journey of searching for her mother. She has tried different approaches, accepted suggestions from other people and even bought things for Geneva as suggested by Miss Davis.

1. Do you consider yourself an open-minded individual? Explain why or why not with examples.

2. Name one advantages and one disadvantages of being open-minded?

3. How is having an open mind important when it comes to achieving your goals?

_____**Answers will vary from learner to learner.**_____

Lesson Four - Answers

This lesson coincides with Chapter 4 of the book, 'Reuniting with Mother'. The purpose of this lesson is to observe and analyze character transformation.
Chapter Four – "Reunited"

Main Idea and Supporting Details

Place an X on the line beside the main idea of the text.

_____ Geneva was not comfortable with meeting Grace's brothers together.

_____**X**_____ **Geneva finally opened up and started talking about some personal things.**

_____ Geneva wanted to know where her other children were as well.

The four statements below "support" the main idea. Fill in the blanks with the correct word.

(a) Geneva told Grace and Terrence that she had **four** more children after she left. (Page 92)

(b) Geneva and Calvin were together for **two** years. (Page 93)

(c) Geneva confirmed that she did not give Grace her middle name, which was **LaJoy**. (Page 94)

(d) Geneva's favorite food was **fried chicken**. (Page 95)

Sequencing

Number the events of Chapter 4 in the order they happened.

(4)   After that, she asked to see Terrence and opened up while he was there. (Page 91)

(2)   The brothers were confused as to why she wanted to see Grayson first. (Page 88)

(5)   She divulged some personal information during that time. (Page 92)

(1)   Geneva agreed to see Grace's brothers one at a time. (Page 87)

(6)   Grace and Terrence decide to come back the next day to have dinner with Geneva. (Page 95)

(3)   Next, Geneva asked to see "Devon" since that's how she remembered him. (Page 89)

Plot Analysis: Falling Action

The falling action happens right after the climax in a story, when the main problem starts to resolve. This is where the tension arising from the story's main conflict starts to decrease. The falling action is also referred to as "Denouement".

In Chapter 4, we have started to see a change in Geneva's attitude towards Grace and her brothers. Compile information from Chapters 1 to 4, and write a brief note on what the climax and falling action is for this story.

Reuniting with Mother	
Climax	**Falling Action**
The climax starts in Chapter 1 when Grace phones the boarding home and talks to Geneva. The following moments are very tense as Grace and her brothers are desperate to confirm if the woman they spoke to was actually their mother. They travel to another state just to confirm this.	Although Geneva wasn't accepting of Grace and her brothers at the beginning, she starts to become more comfortable after Grace shows her pictures and documents of her family. On the second day, she finally allows them to take pictures with her, hug and kiss her, and gives out some personal information that Grace has always wanted to know.

Identifying Cause and Effect

"This was an amazing moment for me, because I had longed to find the siblings my mother had after she left."

What is the Cause? <u>I had longed to find the siblings my mother had after she left.</u>

What is the Effect? <u>This was an amazing moment for me,</u>

Character Transformation

Using the information from Chapters 1-4, write your observations on how Geneva behaved with Grace and her brothers at the beginning, and how she starts to change in Chapter 4.

Geneva	
Before	After
At the beginning, Geneva refused to accept Grace and her siblings because she did not recognize them. She felt uncomfortable, afraid and was not willing to share any personal information.	In chapter 4, she starts to become more comfortable with Grace and agrees to see her brothers one by one. She becomes most comfortable with Terrence and gives out some personal information. She finally warms up and agrees to have dinner with them the following day.

Character Trait Discussion

The character trait for Chapter 4 is "patient".
 Patient means you are able to accept or tolerate delays without getting annoyed easily.

Read the statement below. Then choose <u>one</u> of the questions below and answer it. Write your answer in the space provided then discuss it with your group.

Grace had been tremendously patient with her mother until she agreed to see her brothers one by one.

1. Would you be patient if you were in Grace's situation? Why or why not?

2. Who is the most patient person you know and why?

3. Is it better to be patient and understanding, or be demanding for faster results? Please explain why.

_____**Answers will vary from learner to learner.** _____

_____

_____

_____

_____

Lesson Five - Answers

This lesson coincides with Chapter 5 of the book, 'Reuniting with Mother'. The purpose of this lesson is to study the resolution of the story and interpret the author's intent.
Chapter Five – "Our Final Visit With Mother"

Main Idea and Supporting Details
Place an X on the line beside the main idea of the text.

_____ Grace and her brothers had a chicken dinner with Geneva on the final visit.

_____ Grace wanted to know why Geneva left her and her brothers.

_____X_____ **Grace wishes that Geneva would accept their offers and move to Kansas City.**

The <u>four</u> statements below "support" the main idea. Fill in the blanks with the correct word.

(a) Geneva told Grace that she had some **business** to take care of before she could move. (Page 104)

(b) Terrence told Geneva that if she moved to Kansas City, they could have her **teeth** fixed and take her to all of her **appointments**. (Page 103)

(c) Grace was shocked that Geneva preferred to live in the **poverty-stricken** place she was living. (Page 104)

(d) Geneva had lived in the boarding home for **fifteen** years. (Page 104)

Plot Analysis: Resolution

The resolution in a story happens after the falling action and it typically where the story ends. In the resolution, all the conflicts are resolved and the characters come to an agreement. However, the ending of the story need not always be a happy one. Sometimes authors will end stories in such a way that there are future possibilities for a continuation.

Answer each question briefly to uncover the resolution of this story in Chapter 5.

(a) What agreement did the characters come to at the end of the chapter? (Page 104)

***Answer:* <u>At the end of the chapter, Geneva is more relaxed and comfortable talking to Grace and her brothers. She takes pictures with each of them even though she is embarrassed about her teeth. Grace and her brothers want to help her move to Kansas so that they can take care of all her needs. Before leaving, Terrence tells Geneva that she can call them when she is comfortable and wants to join them.</u>**

(b) Was the ending of "Reuniting with Mother" a happy or sad one? Explain. (Page 103)

Answer: <u>The ending was a happy one since Grace and her brothers were able to reunite with Geneva after forty-nine years. However, Grace is a bit disappointed because Geneva was not ready to move to Kansas City right away.</u>

(c) Do you think there is a possibility for the story to continue in the future? Give reasons. **(Answers may vary from learner to learner.)**

Answer: <u>Yes, I think there is a possibility for the story to continue because we do not know if Geneva would agree to move to Kansas City in the future. A lot can happen following the ending of this chapter, so there is a chance for the series to continue. I would also like to see more interactions between Grace and her brothers with Geneva. Perhaps Geneva will get to meet their families, or maybe even be able to reunite with her other children. It would also be nice to know what happened to Carla. Since there are some unanswered questions, I would like the story to continue.</u>

Identifying Cause and Effect

"We all realized that our hands were somewhat tied since that final decision would have to be hers." (Page 104)

What is the Cause? <u>the final decision of moving to Kansas City would be Geneva's.</u>

What is the Effect? <u>We all realized that our hands were somewhat tied.</u>

Textual Evidence

Cite one example from the text to show that the boarding home was not a good place for Geneva to live happily.

Textual Evidence	Explanation
She wore her black purse strapped around her neck and across her chest. She carried two worn plastic grocery bags, one in each hand.	Geneva mentioned in the previous chapter that people have stolen from her and so she keeps her money safe by putting it in her purse, which she straps around her neck and chest.

Author's Intention

Authors write stories for a variety of reasons. They may want to write the story to get a theme across or even just to teach a moral. It is important to understand the author's purpose for writing the story in order to better understand the text.

Complete the table below to decode the author's intention for writing "Finding Mother After Five Decades" and "Reuniting with Mother".

Name of the Author	Grace LaJoy Henderson
Name(s) of the Book(s)	**Finding Mother, Reuniting with Mother**
Themes in the Story	**love, empathy, expectation vs. reality, abandonment and rejection, knowing the truth, reunion, family, determination**
Main Character's Name	**Grace LaJoy**
Main Character's Traits	**determined, empathetic, caring, patient, responsible, tenacious, grateful**
Main Character's Conflict	**searching for her long-lost mother and wanting to know why she left**
Did the main character resolve the conflict in the end?	**Yes, she did. She finds her mother after forty-nine years in another state.**

Based on the information you wrote in the table above, write a brief note on what you think the author wants you to take from this story.

Sample answer: I believe the author wants us to keep trying for the thing we want very badly to happen, even if it takes a very long time. Grace was tempted to give up searching for her mother when all of her search attempts were unsuccessful. If she had given up, she would not have known how close she was to finding her, and probably would never had met her. Therefore, it is important to have faith and believe that you will get what you are hoping for even if it takes a long time. Never give up on your dream. This is a good take away from the story.

Story Summary

Fill in the boxes below to create a brief summary for "Reuniting with Mother After Five Decades".

What happens at the beginning? Introduce the characters and what they are doing. At the beginning, we see Grace and her brothers preparing to travel in order to reunite with their mother, Geneva. The mood is an anticipatory and anxious one, since they are not sure if the woman is actually their mother. (Page 65)	**What is the main conflict of the story?** When Grace and her brothers arrive at the boarding house where Geneva lives, they have a hard time getting her to accept them. Geneva is uncomfortable and afraid, and refuses to give them any personal information. (Page 72)

What is the main idea of the story?

Grace and her brothers finally find their mother, Geneva, and want to take care of her. (Page 82-86)

How were the characters able to resolve the conflict? Grace was persistent in getting Geneva to talk to her. She showed her pictures of her family and her birth certificate. Then Geneva slowly begins to understand who Grace and her brothers are and opens up. Finally, Geneva meets all the brothers and gives out some personal information that Grace has been wanting to hear. (Page 86)	**What happens at the end of the story?** At the end, Grace and her brothers have a chicken dinner with Geneva and take pictures with her. They express their desires to take care of her and her needs. They tell her that she can move to Kansas City to be near them whenever she is ready. Geneva says she has some business to take care of before she can move to their city. (Page 96)

Character Trait Discussion

The character trait for Chapter 3 is "tenaciousness".
Tenaciousness refers to someone or something that holds on firmly.

Read the statement below. Then choose <u>one</u> of the questions below and answer it. Write your answer in the space provided then discuss it with your group.

Grace's tenaciousness helped her to find her mother although it took forty-nine years.

1. When some goals take longer to achieve, it becomes easier to give up. What would motivate you to be tenacious in this case?

2. Name someone you know who is tenacious? Explain why you think they are tenacious.

3. Are there disadvantages to be being tenacious? If so, what are they?

_____**Answers will vary from learner to learner.**_____

_____

_____

_____

_____

_____

_____

_____

_____

_____

_____

_____

Book 3

After the Reunion

Answer Keys
Chapters 1-12

Lesson One - Answers

> This lesson coincides with Chapter One of the book, "After the Reunion: A Story of Acceptance". The purpose of this lesson is to analyze and evaluate the author's emotions post reuniting with her mother.
> **Chapter One – "Returning Home After the Reunion"**

Main Idea and Supporting Details

Place an "X" on the line beside the "main idea" of the story.

__X__ **Grace felt disturbed and unhappy about finding her mother in deprived conditions.**

_____ Grace was expecting to find her mother in a safe environment.

_____ Grace's mother, Geneva was living in a building with beggars and peddlers.

The four statements below "support" the main idea. Fill in the blanks with the correct word.
(Page 111)

(a) Grace took a few days off work after the **reunion** because she was not feeling well.

(b) Grace was **struggling** with the way her mother was living.

(c) She felt so **downhearted** that she needed someone trustworthy to talk to.

(d) Grace was in shock because she had found her mother living in **poverty**.

Sequencing

The following sentences tell what happens in the story. Read them and number them in the correct order.

(a) Grace emailed Elsie about her reunion with her mother. (Page 113) (**9**)

(b) Grace felt her mother should not be living a deprived life. (Page 112) (**6**)

(c) The woman on the counseling hotline consoled Grace. (Page 112) (**5**)

(d) Grace appreciated the woman's interest in her story. (Page 113) (**8**)

(e) Grace contacted Elsie for information about her sibling's adoption. (Page 111) (**1**)

(f) Grace felt downhearted and needed someone to talk to. (Page 111) (**3**)

(g) Grace did not feel well because of her mother's poor living condition. (Page 111) (**2**)

(h) Grace found a number for a counseling hotline. (Page 111) (**4**)

(i) Grace told the woman she had often thought of starting a homeless shelter. (Page 112) (**7**)

(j) Grace felt hopeful as she waited for a response from Elsie. (Page 113) (**10**)

Plot Analysis

Now That you have put the sentences above in the correct order, write which is the beginning, the climax and the end.

The Beginning: Grace contacted Elsie for information about her sibling's adoption. Grace did not feel well because of her mother's poor living condition. Grace felt downhearted and needed someone to talk to.

The Climax: Grace found a number for a counseling hotline. The woman on the counseling hotline consoled Grace. Grace felt her mother should not be living a deprived life. Grace told the woman she had often thought of starting a homeless shelter. Grace appreciated the woman's interest in her story.

The End: Grace emailed Elsie about her reunion with her mother. Grace felt hopeful as she waited for a response from Elsie.

Point of View

Point of view is the voice or persona that the author creates in order to tell the story.
Which point of view does the author use in this story?

(a) first person   (b) third-person limited   (c) omniscient   (d) objective

Check the line beside the word that describe what type of selection this is:

_____ Fiction

_____X_____ Non-fiction

Identifying Cause and Effect

"With that burden lifted, I felt happy for the rest of the day and was able to return to work the next day feeling refreshed."

What is the Cause? <u>With that burden lifted.</u>

What is the Effect? <u>I felt happy for the rest of the day and was able to return to work the next day feeling refreshed.</u>

Comparing and Contrasting

Compare Grace's feelings before and after having the counseling session.

Her feelings before the session	Her feelings after the session
Grace was sad.	She became happy.
She was hopeless.	She became hopeful.
She was stressed.	She became relaxed as her burden lifted.

Character Analysis

Analyze the main character and describe her with a trait. Support your choice with relevant evidences and examples.

Character Name: Grace / the protagonist / the main character / the author

The character is:	Because
Example: helpful	She wanted to start a homeless shelter.
Sensitive	She could not believe that her mother was living a deprived life.
Caring	She was in search of her siblings.
She was sad.	She needed someone to empathize with her and console her.

Contextual Meaning

Read the following excerpt from the story with the highlighted word. Circle True or False below.

"After a **meticulous** online search, I found the number of a counseling hotline where I could speak with someone freely without revealing my true identity."

The word "meticulous" means careful. (Page 111)   / False

Character Trait Discussion

The Character Trait for Lesson One is "benevolent".
Benevolent means well-meaning and kindly.

Read the statement below. Then choose one of the questions below and answer it. Write your answer in the space provided then discuss it with your group.

Grace is benevolent towards her mother and wants to make her life more comfortable. She feels bad about her mother's deprived living conditions and wants to find her a better place to stay.

1. Are you a benevolent person? What are some acts of kindness that you have done?
2. Mention someone you know that is benevolent. State your reasons.
3. Would you do caring things for a loved one, even if they cannot do things for you? Why or why not?

_____**Answers will vary from learner to learner**_____

Lesson Two - Answers

This lesson coincides with Chapter Two of the book, "After the Reunion: A Story of Acceptance". The purpose of this lesson is to understand the setting and the level of care that the author has for her mother.
Chapter Two – "My Search for a Place for Mother"

Main Idea and Supporting Details
Place an "X" on the line beside the "main idea" of the story.

_____ Grace was ready to remove her mother from the boarding home.

__X__ Grace had always dreamed of finding her mother and taking care of her.

_____ Grace did not expect to find her mother living in such poor conditions.

The <u>four</u> statements below "support" the main idea. Fill in the blanks with the correct word.

(Page 115)

(a) Grace began to think about **moving** her mother from where she was to Kansas City.

(b) **April** warned Grace and her siblings that they were not going to happy when they see her living conditions.

(c) Grace **assumed** that her mother would be more than ready to let them care for her.

(d) Grace began discussing with the boarding home office manager about the type of **facility** that she should be looking for in Kansas City.

Sequencing
Number the following lines from Chapter 2 to put them in the correct order. (Pages 115-117)

__2__　　Grace had been warned that she wouldn't be happy seeing her mother's living condition.

__6__　　She asked for the packet of information to share with her brothers and mother.

__1__　　Ever since she was a little girl, Grace had dreamed of finding her mother.

__5__　　Grace chose the second assisted living center.

__3__　　Grace discussed with April about the required facility for her mother in Kansas City.

__4__　　April provided all the required information to search for an assisted living center for her mother.

Point of View

What is the point of view in Chapter 2? Circle the letter for the correct answer.

(a) first-person (b) second-person (c) third-person

Explain your reason here:

Answer: *The narrator is using the pronouns "I" and "me" when narrating the story. This shows that she is telling the story from her point of view. Therefore, it is the first-person point of view.*

Genre

Check the line beside the term that best describes this chapter.

__**X**__ Personal Narrative

_____ Science Fiction

Author's Purpose

What do you think the author's purpose for this chapter is?

Circle the letter for the correct answer.

(a) To entertain with a story about a woman's search for a place for her mother.
(b) To persuade the reader about looking for safe places for old people.
(c) To inform about an assisted living facility.

Identifying Cause and Effect

"In my search for an assisted living facility for her, a nurse told me that since she has a serious mental illness, she would also be eligible to live in a nursing home."

What is the Cause? <u>since she has a serious mental illness</u>

What is the Effect? <u>she would also be eligible to live in a nursing home</u>

Comparing and Contrasting

Compare and contrast the first and second assisted living facility and fill the graphic organizer.

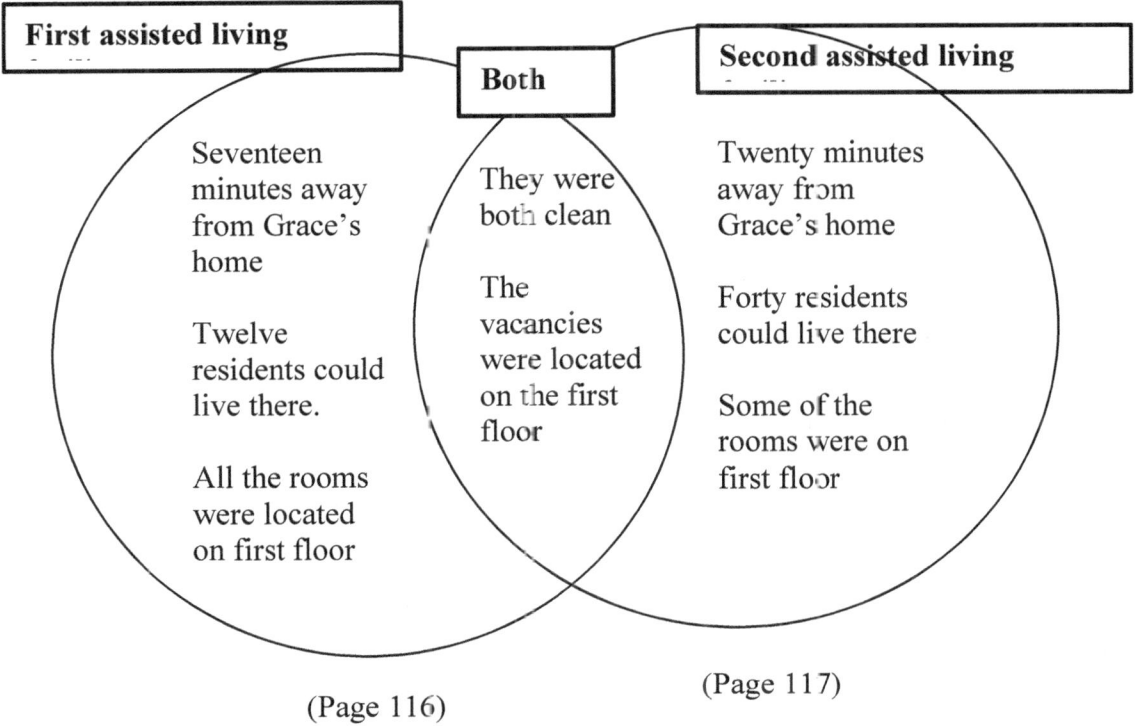

(Page 116) (Page 117)

Interpreting and Evaluating Information

After visiting both places, what made Grace like the second one the best?

Sample answer: <u>Grace found the second assisted living center full of amenities and a better place for her mother as it also had a full-service nursing home. If her mother ever became unable to care for herself, she could move directly to the attached nursing home instead of a new place.</u>

Character Trait Evidence

List five character traits of Geneva, Grace's mother. (Page 116)

(a) <u>elderly</u>

(b) <u>independent</u>

(c) <u>mentally ill</u>

(d) <u>scared</u>

(e) <u>deprived</u>

Contextual Meaning

Read the following line from Chapter 2 with the highlighted word and circle the best meaning for it.

"After the reunion, I continued reviewing the benefits and **amenities** of numerous facilities." What does the word "amenities" mean?"

(a) features　　　　　(b) convenience　　　　　**(c) both a & b**

Character Trait Discussion

The Character Trait for Lesson Two is "thoughtful".
Thoughtful means showing consideration for the needs of other people.

Read the statement below. Then choose one of the questions below and answer it. Write your answer in the space provided then discuss it with your group.

Grace is very thoughtful in finding a comfortable place for her mother to stay. This shows that she is a very caring person.

1. What would you do if you found a long lost relative living in poor conditions?

2. Do you think it is important to look after elderly people? Why or why not?

3. Think about a person you know who is thoughtful? What types of thoughtful things have they done?

_____**Answers will vary from learner to learner.**_____

_____

_____

_____

_____

_____

_____

Lesson Three - Answers

> This lesson coincides with Chapter Three of the book, "After the Reunion: A Story of Acceptance". The purpose of this lesson is to understand the kind of relationship the author has with her mother post reunion through their conversations.
> **Chapter Three – "A Typical Phone Call With Mother"**

Main Idea and Supporting Details

Place an "X" on the line beside the "main idea" of the story.

_____ Geneva made up excuses whenever she wanted to get off the phone.

_____ Grace learned some fun things about her mother when they talked.

__X__ Grace's phone calls with her mother became more frequent as time passed.

The <u>four</u> statements below "support" the main idea. Fill in the blanks with the correct word. (Page 119)

(a) Grace and her mother would initially only talk **once** a month.

(b) After a short while, they would be on the phone every other **week**.

(c) In a later phone conversation, Geneva reminded Grace of her **birthday** and **Christmas**.

(d) Grace felt happy that her mother was able to **communicate** exactly what was important to her.

Sequencing

Read the following extract from Chapter 3 and answer the questions that follow.

"It seemed she was asking me those questions for a few reasons. The first, she may have appreciated me calling her and she enjoyed talking to me. The second, she could have wanted me to feel like she really wanted to talk to me, especially since a lot of the time she would prefer to be in her bed resting her hip. A third, she might have been aiming towards being kind to her daughter whom she knew loved her."

Which words from this extract show sequence?

Answer: <u>first</u>, <u>second</u>, <u>third</u>

Author's Purpose
Which question could best help someone figure out that the author's purpose in this chapter is to entertain?

a) Did the author give me new information?
b) Did the author teach me how to make something?
c) Did the author ask me to do anything?
d) **Did the author tell me a story about her relationship with her mother? (Page 119)**

Identifying Cause and Effect
"Then after a few more words back and forth, she said, "Well, I want to go lay in my bed and rest a little."

What is the Cause? after a few more words back and forth,

What is the Effect? she said, "Well, I want to go lay in my bed and rest a little.

Interpreting and Evaluating Information
Evaluate the mother-daughter relationship in this chapter by analyzing communication.

Sample answer: Initially, Grace would phone her mother once a month to talk. After a while, they would call every week. Grace learned many fun things about her mother and her childhood. She even made sure to send her things on special days since it was important to her mother. Geneva would ask Grace about her day and if she did anything fun. Grace knew what to expect in their conversation, but felt happy that her mother wanted to talk. However, on some days her mother would make up excuses to get off the phone, which made Grace evaluate her mother's feelings about her.

Contextual Meaning
Read the following line from Chapter 2 with the highlighted word and choose the best meaning for it.

"A huge smile would break up on my face before regaining my **composure** enough to say, "Hello, Mother, how are you doing?" (Page 120)

(a) instability   (b) excitement   **(c) self-control**

Character Analysis

Cross out the adjective(s), which are not suitable to describe Grace.

Sensitive	Kind-hearted	excited
Concerned	~~carefree~~	dutiful
Emotional	Caring	~~forgetful~~

Character Trait Discussion

The Character Trait for Lesson Three is "altruistic".
Altruistic means showing a disinterested and selfless concern for the well-being of others.

Read the statement below. Then choose <u>one</u> of the questions below and answer it. Write your answer in the space provided then discuss it with your group.

Grace is altruistic about her mother's needs and phoning to check on her as often as possible.

1. Describe how you communicate with your parent(s). What are some things you do for your parent(s) without being?
2. Do you think it is important to check on family members who are far away? Why or why not?
3. What are some benefits of showing concern for others?

_____**Answers will vary from learner to learner.**_____

Lesson Four - Answers

This lesson coincides with Chapter Four of the book, "After the Reunion: A Story of Acceptance". The purpose of this lesson is to understand the importance of the author's journey for the second time and to analyze the bond she has with her own daughter.
Chapter Four – "My Second Trip to Visit Mother"

Main Idea and Supporting Details
Place an "X" on the line beside the "main idea" of the story.

_____ Grace decided to take her daughter, Arica with her on the trip.

__X__ **Grace decided to visit her mother a second time to find out why she left.**

_____ Jerome was concerned about Grace and Arica driving to Geneva's state.

The <u>four</u> statements below "support" the main idea. Fill in the blanks with the correct word.

(a) Leading up the second trip, Geneva acting very **excited** about Grace coming to visit.
(Page 125)

(b) Grace could not wait for her mother to meet **Arica**. (Page 125)

(c) Grace felt extremely **hopeful** even through Geneva would probably not agree to move.
(Page 126)

(d) Grace and her daughter pulled out many **photos** that she thought Geneva would appreciate.
(Page 127)

Sequencing
Read the following lines from Chapter 4 and put them in the correct order.

(a) They both laughed listened to music. (Page 128)	(9)
(b) Grace was planning to share some information with her mother about assisted living facilities. (Page 125)	(4)
(c) Geneva was very excited about their visit and asked repeatedly about the date of their arrival. (Page 125)	(2)
(d) Grace planned a trip to visit her mother along with her daughter, Arica. (Page 125)	(1)
(e) Grace and her daughter decided to drive a rental car. (Page 126)	(6)
(f) While preparing for the trip, Grace packed some albums. (Page 126)	(7)

(g) Grace was excited and happy at the same time for her mother to meet Arica. (Page 125) (3)

(h) Grace was honored and joyful to receive her daughter's avocado bread. That had
     always been one of her favorite finger foods. (Page 128)   (10)

(i) Terrance pitched in some cash to help them pay for the trip. (Page 126)   (5)

(j) They left the evening before June 8 (Page 127)   (8)

Author's Purpose
An author writes for one of three reasons:
to entertain, to inform (teach) or to persuade (convince)

Circle the author's purpose in this chapter?

(a) to entertain

(b) to inform

(c) to persuade

Explain the reason for your answer:

Answer: The chapters follow all of the story elements and keeps the reader wanting to know more.

Identifying Cause and Effect

"During our reunion visit, I noted that the more she looked at the pictures, the more it began to "click" for her that we were her children. The more she realized we were her children, the more she opened up, and eventually accepted us."

What is the Cause? the more she looked at pictures;

What is the Effect? the more it began to "click" for her that we were her children;

Interpreting and Evaluating Information
What was the purpose of Grace's second visit to her mother?

Sample answer: At the beginning of the chapter, Grace states that the need for answers to her burning questions was a key motivator in wanting to visit her mother for the second time.

Grace also considered this trip to be a mission to get her mother to move back to Kansas City with her, so that they could take care of her.

Comparing and Contrasting

Compare Grace with her daughter Arica and state the similarities between them.

Grace	Similarities	Arica
Grace is Geneva's daughter. Grace drove to visit Geneva.	They are both loving and caring daughters to their mothers.	Arica is Geneva's granddaughter Arica made snacks during the trip.

Language: Idioms

An idiom is a common expression understood figuratively, as the literal meaning makes no sense. Many idioms have been used in this chapter. Write three idioms from Chapter 4.

(a) I felt my breath catch in my throat (Page 125)

(b) pitched in some cash (Page 126)

(c) jog her memory (Page 127)

Inference

Read the short extract from Chapter 4, and place an "X" on the statements that are valid inferences for this extract.

"As I was biting into the delicious snack that my daughter had so carefully prepared, I thought about how grateful I felt that finding my mother had resulted in my sharing this special moment together with my daughter."

___X___ While traveling to visit her mother, Grace and her daughter were having special moments together.

___X___ Traveling to visit her mother ultimately resulted in Grace and her daughter getting time to bond.

_____ Grace was excited for her daughter to meet her grandmother.

_____ Grace and her daughter did not sleep in a motel like Jerome suggested.

Character Analysis
Circle all of the traits that suitable for Grace's brothers: Jerome and Terrence.

Devastated (Helping) (Concerned) (Supportive) Guilt Insecure Excited (Caring)

Character Trait Discussion
The Character Trait for Lesson Four is "loving".
Loving means feeling and showing love or great care.

Read the statement below. Then choose one of the questions below and answer it. Write your answer in the space provided then discuss it with your group.

Grace is loving in the sense that she wants to do everything she can for her mother's well-being and even bring her back home. We can see the same trait in her daughter Arica as well.

1. Describe your relationship with your mother and all things you do together.

2. Why do you think it is important to spend time with your family?

3. If you were in Grace's position, would you drive all the way to visit your mother? Why or why not?

_____**Answers will vary from learner to learner.**_____

_____

_____

_____

_____

_____

_____

_____

_____

Lesson Five - Answers

This lesson coincides with Chapter Five of the book, "After the Reunion: A Story of Acceptance". The purpose of this lesson is to analyze the author's feelings during the second visit to her mother.
Chapter Five – "Arriving on Thursday Evening"

Main Idea and Supporting Details
Place an "X" on the line beside the "main idea" of the story.

___X___ Grace was excited about seeing her mother right away when they arrived.

_____ Grace was happy and proud to finally introduce Arica to her mother.

_____ The photos that Grace brought on the trip captured her mother's attention.

The four statements below "support" the main idea. Fill in the blanks with the correct word.

(a) The **anticipation** of driving to the boarding home where she lived was intense.

(b) Grace was concerned about returning to that **rundown** and **unkempt** neighborhood.

(c) Grace felt that her mother was worth any **inconvenience** that she would experience

to see her.

(d) Geneva did not know the exact **time** that Grace and Arica were coming.

Sequencing
Write briefly in each box what happens in Chapter 5.

Beginning	Middle	End
Grace and Arica arrive on the evening of June 8, and they head straight to the boarding home to visit Geneva.	*Geneva and Arica are introduced to each other. Grace shows her mother all of the pictures she brought and plan to go out for dinner.*	*Since Geneva refused to move to Kansas City, Grace did not show her the assisted living packet. She consults Terrence about it.*

85

Point of View

The passage below is in first person point of view. Rewrite it in the third person point of view.
"It was around five o'clock in the evening of June 7th when we left Kansas City; and it was around five o'clock in the evening of June 8th when we arrived at our out-of-town hotel. Arica and I were both tired and felt like resting, but I was too excited and wanted to go see my mother right away."

Answer: It was around five o'clock in the evening of June 7th when **they** left Kansas City; and it was around five o'clock in the evening of June 8th when **they** arrived at **their** out-of-town hotel. Arica and **Grace** were both tired and felt like resting, but **Grace** was too excited and wanted to go see **her** mother right away.

Author's Purpose
The author's purpose of this selection is to entertain because the author holds readers' attention with enjoyment.

(a) True   (b) False

Identifying Cause and Effect

"She said they had done many nice things to the house, like fixing major holes in the walls and painting. She explained that she was used to being there. Furthermore, she expressed that she did not want to leave at this time. Although I was saddened, I understood how she felt, and most of all, I truly appreciated her honesty."

What is the Cause? they had done many nice things to the house, like fixing major holes in the walls and painting

What is the Effect? she expressed that she did not want to leave at this time

Literary Techniques: Descriptive Language
Write the author's descriptions for the boarding home in the boxes below.

Scenery and View	Scents and Smells
an old non-functional fireplace a large television mounted on the wall two long couches, and some chairs. the living room was organized the walls were free of flaws the floor was clean.	an unbearable odor
Sounds and Noises	**Sensation and Surface**
Loud and noisy	The living room featured brown hardwood floors.

Character Analysis
Grace was having a mixture of feelings at different parts of the story.
Analyze Grace's emotions before and after meeting her mother again.

Before	After
Grace was very excited to meet her mother for the second time. She did not even want to rest after arriving in her mother's state. She did not like traveling on those hectic roads to reach the boarding home, but her mother was worth any inconvenience for her.	Although the meeting with her mother went well, she felt disappointed that her mother refused to leave the boarding home at the time. She also felt a sense of abandonment when her mother took some time to return with the photo of Danisha.

Character Trait Discussion
The Character Trait for Lesson Five is "accommodating".
Accommodating means willing to fit someone's wishes or needs.

Read the statement below. Then choose one of the questions below and answer it. Write your answer in the space provided then discuss it with your group.
Grace is very accommodating towards her mother. She does not pressure her into moving to Kansas City even though she would like her to. Yet, she continues to care for her mother.

1. What would you do to convince your mother to move closer to you?

2. Do you think it is better to respect someone's wishes to stay where they are, or compel them to move because the place is bad? Explain your answer.

3. Think of an accommodating person who you know and explain why you feel that person is accommodating.

_____**Answers will vary from learner to learner.**_____

Lesson Six

This lesson coincides with Chapter Six of the book, "After the Reunion: A Story of Acceptance". The purpose of this lesson is to analyze the author's mother and her connection with the people around her.

Chapter Six – "Day Two of Our Visit - Friday"

Main Idea and Supporting Details

Place an "X" on the line beside the "main idea" of the story.

_____ Donna was shocked to know that Grace and Arica were Geneva's family.

__X__ **Grace thought about the fun they would have participating in activities with Geneva.**

_____ All the workers thought that Geneva was nice, quiet and didn't bother anyone.

The four statements below "support" the main idea. Fill in the blanks with the correct word.

(a) Geneva told Grace and Arica to come to the **center** around noon. (Page 139)

(b) When they arrived at the address, they met the center manager, **Donna**. (Page 139)

(c) Donna gave Grace her **cellular phone number** and welcomed her to call anytime. (Page 140)

(d) Grace felt **embarrassed** for expecting to participate in activities with Geneva at the center. (Page 141)

Character Analysis: Geneva

Analyze Geneva's character by giving her two traits based on this chapter. Support your choice by citing relevant examples from the text.

Traits	Example from the Text
Scared / Fearful	Donna said she had to remind my mother that if she did not take her medication that she could end up locked up in a mental hospital again. Having a fear of going back there, she started taking it regularly.
Moody / Unpredictable	Not realizing we had already told Donna who we were, my mother told her that it was none of her business.

Identifying Cause and Effect

"She mentioned they recently had some difficulty getting her to take it consistently. She told me a story of how the workers noticed she had been acting angry and cussing at people more than usual. The staff came up with a bright idea to check under the mattress on her bed. There they found the pills she was supposed to be taking daily, but she had been hiding them instead. Donna said she had to remind my mother that if she did not take her medication that she could end up locked up in a mental hospital again. Having a fear of going back there, she started taking it regularly."

What is the Cause? <u>Having a fear of going back to the hospital</u>

What is the Effect? <u>she started taking it her pills regularly</u>

-or-

What is the Cause? <u>she had been hiding her medication instead of taking them</u>

What is the Effect? <u>she was acting angry and cussing at people more than usual</u>

Interpreting and Evaluating Information
What are the things that Donna liked about Geneva?

Sample answer: <u>Just like everyone else, Donna too thought that Geneva was nice, quiet and did not bother anyone. She says that Geneva was all those things as long as she took her medication properly. She also states that the things that impressed her the most about Geneva was the fact that she does not touch drugs even though she is around them.</u>

Contextual Meaning
Read the following line from Chapter 6 with the highlighted word and choose the best meaning for it.

"I woke up the next morning, **envisioning** the fun we would have sitting in the center, participating in activities with my mother."

(a) disregarding   (b) neglecting   **(c) visualizing**

Character Trait Discussion

The Character Trait for Lesson Six is "acquiescent".

Acquiescent means ready to accept something without protest, or to do what someone else wants.

Read the statement below. Then choose one of the questions below and answer it. Write your answer in the space provided then discuss it with your group.

Grace is acquiescent in regard to her mother's needs. She arrives at the center hoping to participate in activities with her mother.

1. Would you be willing to participate in activities with an elderly person?

    Explain why or why not.

2. Have you ever been acquiescent just to please someone? Describe the situation.

3. Do you think it good to be acquiescent all the time? Discuss you answer.

_____**Answers will vary from learner to learner.**_____

Lesson Seven - Answers

This lesson coincides with Chapter Seven of the book, "After the Reunion: A Story of Acceptance". The purpose of this lesson is to analyze the author's mother and her connection with the people around her.
Chapter Seven – "Day Two of Our Visit – Talking with Mother"

Main Idea and Supporting Details
Place an "X" on the line beside the "main idea" of the story.

___X___ Geneva talks about her husband and the birth order of all her children.

_____ Geneva is concerned about Carla missing.

_____ Grace was surprised to hear that her father had been traveling even before Geneva left.

The four statements below "support" the main idea. Fill in the blanks with the correct word.

(a) Geneva and Grace's father moved to another state and lived there for **eight** years. (Page 144)

(b) Geneva told Arica that her husband was **nice** and **helpful** to her. (Page 145)

(c) Geneva remembered buying a **toy oven** for Carla. (Page 147)

(d) Geneva did not remember buying Grace chocolate covered **malt balls**. (Page 147)

Literary Devices: Flashback
Flashbacks are interruptions that writers do to insert past events, in order to provide background or context to the current events of a narrative.
Cite two examples of flashbacks from this chapter.

Example 1:	Example 2:
Then she continued her story, "So after I got my job, I worked there for two years. Then that's when I met my husband. There was a girl who worked at the same place where I worked. So, she asked me 'You want to come over my sister's house with me?' I said, 'Yeah, I'll go.' So, at her sister's house, that is where I met my husband."	She remembered buying a toy oven for Carla. "It had a little stove and a little sink and you put the water in the back in a container. Then you'd turn on the faucet and the water really came out of the faucet. Carla loved that! She would say, 'Mommy, help me bake a cake.' So, it baked little cakes and cookies and they loved that."

Literary Elements: Tone
The tone is the feeling or the atmosphere set by the author. What is author's tone in this chapter? Circle the letter for the correct answer.

(a) gloomy   (b) ironic   **(c) nostalgic**

Identifying Cause and Effect

"Right. It's a nice place to live for now. You never know what's going to happen when you look ahead, you know. Right now, you know, I'd rather stay here, you know."

What is the Cause? You never know what's going to happen when you look ahead,

What is the Effect? Right now, you know, I'd rather stay here,

Interpreting and Evaluating Information
Write two reasons why Grace's father left her and his siblings alone at home. (Pages 145-146)

Reason 1: **In order to support his big family, Grace's father would constantly travel for work.**

Reason 2: **He needed to work in order to provide for his family and keep them together.**

Contextual Meaning
Read the following line from Chapter 7 with the highlighted word and circle the best meaning for it.

"I found that **intriguing**. I asked her if she remembered walking me to a convenience store in Kansas City."

(a) fascinating   (b) uninteresting   (c) boring

Inference
What can you infer from the following lines?

"Right. It's a nice place to live for now. You never know what's going to happen when you look ahead, you know. Right now, you know, I'd rather stay here, you know." (Page 148)

Sample answer: We understand that Geneva is content where she is because she has been living at the boarding house for fifteen years, contributing to its upkeep. It is apparently a place close to her heart. However, she does not completely refuse Grace's offer to move to Kansas City.

Character Trait Discussion

The Character Trait for Lesson Seven is "affable".
Affable means friendly, good-natured and easy to talk to.

Read the statement below. Then choose one of the questions below and answer it. Write your answer in the space provided then discuss it with your group.

Geneva was affable with Grace and Arica during their time together. She did not make them feel unwelcome or uncomfortable during their conversation.

1. Are you an affable person? Explain why or why not.

2. Mention someone you can talk about anything with. State at least one reason.

3. What are two benefits of being an affable person?

_____**Answers will vary from learner to learner.**_____

_____

_____

_____

_____

_____

_____

_____

_____

_____

_____

_____

_____

Lesson Eight - Answers

This lesson coincides with Chapter Eight of the book, "After the Reunion: A Story of Acceptance". The purpose of this lesson is to study some background information in order to understand the author's mother better.
Chapter Eight – "Day Two of Our Visit – Talking About Moving"

Main Idea and Supporting Details
Place an "X" on the line beside the "main idea" of the story.

_____ Geneva told Grace and Arica some stories of her childhood.

__X__ **Grace showed Geneva the information on the facility she had picked for her.**

_____ Grace was not ready to take long-distance responsibility for her mother.

The four statements below "support" the main idea. Fill in the blanks with the correct word.

(a) **Terrence** had insisted that Grace show Geneva the information about the facility.

 (Page 149)

(b) Grace pulled out a **folder** which contained all the information. (Page 149)

(c) Grace told Geneva that she can leave her **belongings** in her own room at the

 facility because they would be safe. (Page 149)

(d) Geneva stated that the facility looked like **luxury** and that she was not ready for anything

 like that. (Page 151)

Character Analysis
What can you tell about the Geneva's character based on the childhood stories she told Arica?

Geneva's Childhood	
Who were her family?	Mother and father (Page 155)
What were some activities she indulged in?	Bike riding on the street, skating (Page 156 &157)
Was she an obedient or mischievous child? Explain why.	She was mischievous because she rode the bike and hurt her knee when her mother told her not to. She even brought home someone else's skates that were on the street. (Page 157)

Identifying Cause and Effect

"I felt surprised, yet grateful when Arica asked the question about how Mother felt when she met us."

What is the Cause? <u>when Arica asked the question about how Mother felt when she met us.</u>

What is the Effect? <u>I felt surprised, yet grateful</u>

Interpreting and Evaluating Information
Mention three ways in which Grace tried to convince her mother to move to Kansas City.

Grace tells Geneva that the facility would be exactly like the one she is living in, except she would have her own room.
She would not have to carry her belongings around in a backpack for fear of them being stolen.
All utilities were included except phones, and she could even take part in many activities. There was even a hairdresser at the facility.

Comparing and Contrasting
Compare Geneva's condition with and without her medication.

With Medication	Without Medication
Geneva is nice and does not bother anybody when she takes her medication.	Her behavior becomes uncontrollable when she does not take her medication.

Character Trait Discussion
The Character Trait for Lesson Eight is "enthusiastic".
Enthusiastic means showing intense interest and excitement.

Read the statement below. Then choose <u>one</u> of the questions below and answer it. Write your answer in the space provided then discuss it with your group.

At the beginning of the chapter, Grace is enthusiastic about sharing the information about the facility she picked for her mother. She hopes that her mother would be convinced to move.

1. Name one thing that you have been enthusiastic about sharing with your family?

2. Name 3 things you are enthusiastic about?

3. Do you think it is important to be enthusiastic? Why or why not?

_____**Answers will vary from learner to learner.**_____

_____
_____
_____
_____
_____
_____
_____
_____
_____
_____
_____
_____

Lesson Nine - Answers

This lesson coincides with Chapter Nine of the book, "After the Reunion: A Story of Acceptance". The purpose of this lesson is to observe some similarities the author has with her mother.
Chapter Nine – "Day Three of Our Visit - Saturday"

Main Idea and Supporting Details
Place an "X" on the line beside the "main idea" of the story.

_____ Geneva bought some soda pop for Grace and Arica.

_____ Grace had forgotten to make the video call with Terrence and Grayson.

___X___ **Grace was able to observe her mother and understand where she got certain traits and features from.**

The <u>four</u> *statements below "support" the main idea. Fill in the blanks with the correct word.*

(a) Grace noticed her mother walking on her **tiptoes**. (Page 161)

(b) Grace also noticed that her **sense of humor** was similar to her mother's. (Page 162)

(c) Grace and her mother laughed at each other's **witticisms**. (Page 162)

(d) Realizing where she got some of her **features** and **characteristics** from made Grace appreciate herself more. (Page 162)

Summarizing
Summarize the following paragraph in two sentences.

"After a while, Mother finally entered the living room with a big smile on her face. Her backpack was in one hand, and two bottles of soda pop was in the other. She held the necks of the bottles in between her fingers. The proud look on her face indicated that she was confident we would be happy about getting the drinks; and that we would feel it was worth the wait to quench our thirst at last."

Sample answer: <u>Geneva bought two bottles of soda pop for Grace and Arica. She felt proud and confident that they would enjoy the drinks and feel it was worth the wait to quench their thirst.</u>

Identifying Cause and Effect

"After that, I made a regular voice call to Terrance and found out he had already left Grayson's house. They had waited for my call for an hour, then gave up. I told him how sorry I was and that if he went back around to Grayson's house, I would call again. He assured me it was okay and said he did not have time to go back over."

What is the Cause? <u>They had waited for my call for an hour, then gave up.</u>

What is the Effect? <u>I told him how sorry I was and that if he went back around to Grayson's house, I would call again.</u>

Comparing and Contrasting

Compare Geneva and Grace by stating the similarities between them.

Geneva	Similarities	Grace
	• *They both did not pick up their feet when they walked.* • *They both walked on their tiptoes.* • *They had a similar sense of humor.*	

Interpreting and Evaluating Information

Explain what Geneva meant when she said that she would feel embarrassed about "hopping" into the restaurant.

Sample answer: <u>Geneva had been suffering with a hip problem which caused her to limp when she walked. Therefore, when Grace reminded her that they would be taking her out to dinner, Geneva expressed that she would feel embarrassed to "hop" into the restaurant. She meant that she was not able to walk properly and felt uncomfortable about it.</u>

Character Trait Analysis: Geneva

In this chapter, we learn more about Geneva's character and personality. Describe Geneva's character by stating some traits for her and supporting them with evidences.

Traits	Examples
hospitable	"She told me she had given a young man some money and sent him to the store to buy Arica and me some bottles of soda pop."
puzzled	"When she finally saw us, she looked a little puzzled to realize we had been sitting there without her being aware we were there."
shy / hesitant	"She mentioned that she would be embarrassed about "hopping" into the restaurant due to her hip pain."

Character Trait Discussion

The Character Trait for Lesson Nine is "appreciation".
Appreciation means recognition and enjoyment of the good qualities of someone or something.

Read the statement below. Then choose one of the questions below and answer it. Write your answer in the space provided then discuss it with your group.
Grace appreciated herself more after noticing some similarities between herself and her mother.

1. Describe three things that you appreciate about yourself and explain why.

2. Who do you appreciate the most in your life and why?

3. Do you feel it is better to appreciate the things we have and not complain? Why or why not?

_____**Answers will vary from learner to learner.**_____

_____

_____

_____

Lesson Ten - Answers

This lesson coincides with Chapter Ten of the book, "After the Reunion: A Story of Acceptance". The purpose of this lesson is to observe the author's feelings and reaction to an unexpected turn or events.
Ten – "Day Four of Our Visit - Sunday"

Main Idea and Supporting Details
Place an "X" on the line beside the "main idea" of the story.

_____ Grace bought Geneva some new and comfortable sandals.
__**X**__ **Grace felt disappointed that Geneva refused to go out to dinner.**
_____ Everyone at the boarding home acted like they didn't know Geneva had children.

The <u>four</u> statements below "support" the main idea. Fill in the blanks with the correct word.

(a) Grace woke up feeling very **excited** on Sunday morning. (Page 163)

(b) She was planning to strike up the **conversation** at dinner about why Geneva left

forty-nine years ago. (Page 163)

(c) For months, since their **reunion** Grace had been looking forward to talking to

Geneva about it. (Page 163)

(d) Grace excitement **evaporated** when Geneva said that she wasn't going to dinner with them.

(Page 164)

Story Elements: Dialogue
Read the following dialogues from Chapter 10 and write who said it.

"You all are early."	**Geneva** (Page 164)
"Do you want to sit where we were sitting yesterday?"	**Geneva** (Page 166)
"Geneva, I didn't know you had children!"	**woman** (Page 165)
"How do those feel?"	**Grace** (Page 167)
"I am *her* daughter!"	**Grace** (Page 165)
"Did you hear from Terrance?"	**Geneva** (Page 167)
"I'm not going!"	**Geneva** (Page 164)

Identifying Cause and Effect

"I went to the car and came back to the front of the house with the shopping bag in my hand. I took out the items and showed them to her. She tried on the shoes and said they were very comfortable. She really liked them a lot."

What is the Cause? <u>I took out the items and showed them to her.</u>

What is the Effect? <u>She tried on the shoes and said they were very comfortable. She really liked them a lot.</u>

Reading for Information
Scan the text to find the answer for the question below.
What did Grace buy for Geneva while shopping in the city?

Answer: <u>She bought some sandals and socks for her.</u> (Page 164)

Contextual Meaning
Read the following line from Chapter 10 with the highlighted word and choose the best meaning for it.

"I couldn't help but marvel at the way she was **cognizant** about the time of day."

(a) unaware   **(b) conscious**   (c) ignorant

Character Trait Discussion
The Character Trait for Lesson Ten is "understanding".
Understanding means having sympathetic awareness or tolerance.

Read the statement below. Then choose <u>one</u> of the questions below and answer it. Write your answer in the space provided then discuss it with your group.

Although disappointed, Grace was understanding when her mother refused to go to dinner because of her hip problem.

1. How would you react if you made plans with someone and they backed out at the last minute?

2. Would you consider yourself an understanding person? Explain why or why not.

3. Do you think it is better to be understanding and not angry when someone does not cooperate with you? Why or why not?

_____**Answers will vary from learner to learner.**_____

Lesson Eleven - Answers

This lesson coincides with Chapter Eleven of the book, "After the Reunion: A Story of Acceptance". The purpose of this lesson is to analyze past events in order to understand the current situation in the stoty.
Chapter Eleven – "Day Four of Our Visit – Why Mother Left"

Main Idea and Supporting Details
Place an "X" on the line beside the "main idea" of the story.

_____ Grace felt nervous about asking her mother to talk about why she left.

_____ Grace's father never visited Geneva when she was put in a mental hospital.

__X__ Grace was relieved that Arica's questions made Geneva talk about why she left.

The four statements below "support" the main idea. Fill in the blanks with the correct word.

(a) Geneva said that she was a **private** person when Grace asked her about why she left.
  (Page 169)

(b) Geneva totally **disregarded** Grace's request to go outside and talk. (Page 170)

(c) Arica's plea had genuinely touched Geneva's **emotions**. (Page 171)

(d) Geneva understood how **important** it was for her to open up and share her story. (Page 171)

Sequencing
Put the following dialogues from this chapter in the correct order. (Page 169-173)

__1__	"I'm a private person."
__10__	"I would come home on furlough."
__2__	"I feel like I know. I just want to hear you say the actual words."
__6__	"Yes, that's the same one,"
__9__	"He was nice to me. He just wanted me to feel better."
__7__	"Right. Well uh,"
__3__	"Can she hear us?"
__4__	"When we be on the phone, she eavesdrops and then she will gossip. So, I don't want to come right out with anything. You know?"
__8__	"He and grandmother told me you left and you did not want me. But, even if that was the case, I forgive you."
__5__	"Now or never."

Character Analysis
Describe Grace's psychological state when she tries to ask her mother to share her story about why she left forty-nine years ago.
Sample answer: Grace feels disappointed, disheartened and frustrated when her mother does not answer her questions about why she left many years ago. Grace had traveled all the way from Kansas City to meet her mother and get this information from her first-hand. However, when her mother does not readily share her story, Grace can't help but feel saddened by this.

Literary Elements: Theme
The Theme is the message that author wants to convey.

What is the theme of this selection?
(a) reunion   (b) denial   **(c) rejection**

Identifying Cause and Effect
"It all began before you were born. I would often feel tired from taking care of the five kids your father and I had together. He would go out of town for work, leaving me alone with them for one or two weeks at a time. I told him I needed a break from the kids…"

What is the Cause? He would go out of town for work, leaving me alone with them for one or two weeks at a time.

What is the Effect? I would often feel tired from taking care of the five kids your father and I had together.

Interpreting and Evaluating Information
What kind of relationship did Geneva have with her husband?

Sample answer: Geneva seemed to have had a very painful and unhealthy relationship with her husband. He did not talk to her much, but would abuse and hit her whenever she did something wrong. However, Geneva loved him and taught her children to love their father.

Character Trait Discussion
The Character Trait for Lesson Eleven is "inquisitive".
Inquisitive means having or showing an interest in learning things.

Read the statement below. Then choose one of the questions below and answer it. Write your answer in the space provided then discuss it with your group.

Grace was very inquisitive in learning from Geneva the reason for her leaving.

1. What are some things you are inquisitive about right now? Explain why.
2. What would you do if someone was inquisitive about a secret you have kept for a long time?
3. Should one be inquisitive rather than mind their own business? Discuss.

_____**Answers will vary from learner to learner.**_____

Lesson Twelve - Answers

This lesson coincides with Chapter Twelve of the book, "After the Reunion: A Story of Acceptance". The purpose of this lesson is to analyze the author's feelings after visiting her mother.

Chapter Twelve – "Day Four of Our Visit – Returning Home"

Main Idea and Supporting Details

Place an "X" on the line beside the "main idea" of the story.

_____ Grace wishes that Geneva would agree to move to Kansas City.

__X__ The trip had served its purpose for Grace as Geneva answered some questions.

_____ Geneva was perfectly happy with where she was staying.

The four statements below "support" the main idea. Fill in the blanks with the correct word. (Page 181)

(a) Grace did a lot of **thinking** about how she felt the visit had gone.

(b) She **appreciated** her mother for doing the best she could to talk about why she left.

(c) Geneva was in **denial** about a lot of the ways she was feeling back then.

(d) Grace **valued** the things that Geneva felt comfortable sharing, but **doubtful** that she had truly given her all the facts.

Sequencing

Put the following dialogues in order from Chapter 12. (Page 179-180)

____8____	"Wow, I am much prettier than I thought I was!"
____1____	"Yes, I'm okay."
____7____	"That sounds good!"
____4____	"You only shared what you were comfortable with right?"
____6____	"They don't read it!"
____2____	"Miss. Geneva, this is heavy! How do you do it?"
____5____	"Did you play the piano?"
____3____	"I'm a strong woman, you just don't know!"

Literary Elements: Theme
What is the dominating theme in this chapter?

(a) rejection	(b) denial	**(c) reunion**

Figurative Language: Symbolism

Symbolism is anything that stands for something other than its literal meaning.
In the chapter, Geneva's "backpack" has been mentioned various times. Arica even says that it is very heavy. What do you think it symbolized?

Sample answer: The backpack could have been a symbol for all of the painful memories and emotions of not having a family that Geneva had been keeping with her for years. As she had kept all those things to herself, her burden became heavier as years passed. Therefore, the backpack is compared to her memories and emotions of her painful past. Geneva responds to Arica by saying she is a very strong woman. Perhaps she meant that she was strong enough to carry all of those emotions, rather than being physically strong.

Inference
What do you infer from the following line in Chapter 12?
"My heart wept for her at that moment."

Sample answer: It means that Grace felt sorry for Geneva that she was not able to keep any of her children. When Geneva found the house where her other four children was living boarded up, she was devastated. She knew what had happened to them. Grace could relate as she too had been taken away when her father had left her and her siblings alone in the house. Therefore, she is empathizing with Geneva here.

Character Analysis

Analyze Geneva's character. She has been given three traits. Define those traits in your own words and quote evidences from the text.

Trait	Definition	Evidences
religious	a person who practices religion	"They even stole my Bible! Can you imagine who would want to steal a Bible? They don't read it!" (Page 179)
strong	able to withstand	"I'm a strong woman, you just don't know!" (Page 179)
pretty	beautiful	"Wow, I am much prettier than I thought I was!" (Page 180)

Comparing and Contrasting

Compare Grace's feelings before and after the second trip.

Before	After
Grace was very excited and hopeful about meeting Geneva. She thought that Geneva was answer all of her queries about why she left so long ago, and also that she would agree to move to Kansas City.	Grace felt satisfied that Geneva that at least answered her queries partially. However, she felt disappointed and disheartened that Geneva did not want to move to Kansas City.

Character Trait Discussion

The Character Trait for Lesson Twelve is "accepting".
Accepting means taking or receiving something with approval or favor.

Read the statement below. Then choose one of the questions below and answer it. Write your answer in the space provided then discuss it with your group.

In this chapter, Grace is accepting the fact that her mother is happy staying where she is. She also accepts that Geneva left on her own accord.

1. Would you be accepting of someone who does something wrong to you?

2. Do you think it is better to be accepting and tolerant rather than impatient with others?

Why or why not?

3. Would you accept a loved one's wishes even if it did not make you happy? Why or why not?

_____**Answers will vary from learner to learner.**_____

Book 4

Diary of Emotions

Answer Keys
30 Entries

Lesson One - Answers

This lesson coincides with a diary entry dated July 20, 2018 from "Diary of Emotions: Thoughts and Feelings". The purpose of this lesson is to analyze the main character's feelings and emotions after the main event took place.
Entry Date: July 20, 2018

Main Idea and Supporting Details
Place an "X" on the line beside the "main idea" of the story.

_____ Grace has accepted that her mother has a mental illness.

__X__ Grace cannot understand how a mother can abandon her children.

_____ Grace wants to provide for and take care of her mother.

The <u>four</u> statements below "support" the main idea. Fill in the blanks with the correct word.

(a) Even though her mother left, Grace had completely **forgiven** her.

(b) For years, Grace did not **blame** her mother for leaving her and her siblings.

(c) I However, Grace finds it hard to **fathom** how a mother could not want to be close to her children.

(d) It hurts Grace that her mother has **mental problems** to the point where she does not want her children.

Plot Analysis: Internal Conflict

In a story, an internal conflict is a battle taking place within the mind of a character. This is also referred to as the "man vs. self" conflict.

In this diary entry, we see Grace having an internal conflict regarding her mother. Which statement shows Grace's internal conflict? Circle the letter for the correct one.

(a) It is weird that my mother can leave me and I can still forgive her.
(b) A part of me wants to do things for her all the time, to take care of her.
(c) Still, I do not know how to feel about her.
(d) I know she was not capable of raising us....it still makes me want to accuse her of something.

Analyzing Characters and Incidents
In the boxes below, write three different lines from the diary entry that show Grace is saddened by her mother rejecting her.

> *Seeing that she does not want to be with us, I feel like I should place some of the blame on her.*

> *Still it hurts that my mother has mental problems to the point where she does not want her children.*

> *It is hard to fathom how a mother could not want to be close to her children.*

Identifying Cause and Effect

"Seeing that she does not want to be with us, I feel like I should place some of the blame on her."

What is the Cause? <u>Seeing that she does not want to be with us,</u>

What is the Effect? <u>I feel like I should place some of the blame on her.</u>

Drawing Conclusions
Read the following statement from the diary entry and choose the best conclusion for it.

"Like if I do not call her, we do not talk. If I stopped calling her, I would never hear from her again, even though she has my phone number. Then again, it may be for the best."

(a) Grace feels that her mother does not want to talk to her at all.

(b) Grace feels hurt that her mother does not get in touch on her own, but accepts it.

(c) Grace knows that her mother has a mental illness, but does not understand the reason for her mother's shyness.

(d) Grace is angry with her mother for not calling on her own even though she has their phone numbers.

Character Trait Discussion

The Character Trait for Lesson One is "forgiving".
Forgiving means being ready and willing to forgive.

Read the statement below. Then choose <u>one</u> of the questions below and answer it. Write your answer in the space provided then discuss it with your group.
In this diary entry, we see Grace's forgiving side as she says she had forgiven her mother for years.

1. Would you forgive someone who left you ages ago and reunited with them again? Why or why not?

2. Describe a situation where you had to forgive someone, or where you were the one seeking forgiveness.

3. Do you think it is difficult for some people to forgive? Why or why not.

_____**Answer will vary from learner to learner.**_____

_____

_____

_____

_____

_____

_____

_____

_____

_____

_____

_____

Lesson Two - Answers

This lesson coincides with a diary entry dated August 11, 2018 from "Diary of Emotions: Thoughts and Feelings". The purpose of this lesson is to understand the reason for the mother's attitude towards the main character.
Entry Date: August 11, 2018

Main Idea and Supporting Details
Place an "X" on the line beside the "main idea" of the story.

_____ Grace wants to send her mother a few things, which will be useful for her.

_____ Grace wishes she could have a normal relationship with her mother.

__X___ Grace feels hurt that her mother did not want to talk to her.

The <u>four</u> statements below "support" the main idea. Fill in the blanks with the correct word.

(a) It had been a few **weeks** since the last time Grace talked with her mother.

(b) Grace suspected that her mother had not been taking her **medication**.

(c) Grace assumed that her mother may not be **comfortable** communicating with anybody.

(d) Grace understands that her mother is not **capable** of doing anything for anyone.

Point of View: Objective vs. Subjective Narrator
*The **objective narrator** is a mere observer in the story and cannot enter into the minds of the other characters, except in a speculative way. This narrator is like a reporter on the scene of an event transpiring.*

*The **subjective narrator** on the other hand, knows everything about a single character and can see the story through the eyes of that character.*

Read the following statement and decide if the narrator is objective or subjective in nature.

I felt like maybe that might have been her way of saying, "Even though I enjoy these phone calls, I just do not care much for being on the phone."

(a) Objective point of view
(b) Subjective point of view

Making Inferences

An inference is an idea or conclusion that is taken from evidence and reasoning.
Based on your understanding of the text, answer the question below in a sentence or more.

How would you describe the relationship between Grace and her mother in this entry?

Sample answer: Grace wishes that she could have a normal relationship with her mother even though they are estranged. We see Grace regularly keeping in touch to check on her mother despite not receiving the same affection from the other side. Grace tries to hide her frustration and hurt, and continues to care for her mother by sending her necessary things because she somewhat accepts that her mother is not capable of doing anything for her.

Analyzing Characters and Incidents

Circle the letter for the correct statement.

Why didn't Grace's mother want to come to the phone?

(a) She was probably actually busy with something.

(b) She did not feel like talking to anybody.

(c) Her hip was hurting badly.

(d) She was uncomfortable talking on the phone since she has been on her own for so long.

Identifying Cause and Effect

"I guess a part of me wants to support her in a bigger way, but when I call her and she says she does not feel like talking to anyone, well then, I feel like I should just let her have her life, you know?"

What is the Cause? when I call her and she says she does not feel like talking to anyone,

What is the Effect? I feel like I should just let her have her life,

Character Trait Discussion
The Character Trait for Lesson Two is "understanding".
Understanding in this case means having sympathetic awareness or tolerance.

Read the statement below. Then choose <u>one</u> of the questions below and answer it. Write your answer in the space provided then discuss it with your group.
In this diary entry, Grace shows how understanding she is of her mother not wanting to talk to her by analyzing her feelings.

1. What are some ways in which you can show a person that you understand how they feel?

2. Describe a situation where your patience and understanding solved the problem.

3. Do you know someone who is tolerant with other people? Describe them.

_____**Answers will vary from learner to learner.**_____

_____

_____

_____

_____

_____

_____

_____

_____

_____

_____

_____

Lesson Three - Answers

> This lesson coincides with a diary entry dated August 12, 2018 from "Diary of Emotions: Thoughts and Feelings". The purpose of this lesson is to identify some major themes in the text.
> **Entry Date:** August 12, 2018

Main Idea and Supporting Details
Place an "X" on the line beside the "main idea" of the story.

    _____ Grace is confused about being responsible for her mother's care.
    __**X**__ **Grace yearns to somehow take care of her mother and help her.**
    _____ Grace is thankful for her grandmother because she guided her properly.

The four statements below "support" the main idea. Fill in the blanks with the correct word.

(a) Grace wants to make sure her mother gets treatment for her **hip** because she is always in pain. (Page 200)

(b) Grace looked online and found a **hip brace** that her mother could use. (Page 200)

(c) Grace wishes to serve her mother **healthy meals** and oversee her **medication**. (Page 204)

(d) In addition to taking her out for walks, she wants to take her mother to the **park**. (Page 205)

Literary Elements: Theme
In any literary work, the theme is the underlying message that the writer would like to get across. Circle all the themes that you can find in this diary entry.

(a) identity crisis

(b) longing for escape

(c) facing reality

(d) self-reliance

(e) acceptance

(f) rejection

Character Analysis

Read the following line from the entry and answer the question.

"Just thinking about my mother and a part of me says that is cool if she does not want to be with us, I haven't been with her all my life anyway. I know she has a mental illness, and that she is happy where she is. I feel like the biggest part of me does not really care. Then, there is that part of me that does care and that is the part of me that is talking right now."

Describe Grace's feelings in regard to her mother.

Sample answer: Grace feels confused because of her mother's desire to be on her own, in a state away from her. Although the distance and disconnection tempts her to stop caring, another side of her wants to relentlessly provide for and take care of her mother. She also accepts that her mother has a mental illness and is happy where she. Grace knows that it is important for her mother to be comfortable in order to be happy. Thus, she lets her stay at the boarding home and decides to care for her from a distance.

Identifying Cause and Effect

"I do not remember our utilities being turned off while my father was around. But, after he left us in the house alone, the utilities were disconnected due to nonpayment. I remember not having a phone even with my father around. I remember thinking, "When I grow up and get my own place, I am going to always have a phone, and my bills will always be paid."

What is the Cause? after he left us in the house alone, the utilities were disconnected due to nonpayment

What is the Effect? I remember thinking, "When I grow up and get my own place, I am going to always have a phone, and my bills will always be paid

Reading for Information

Grace mentions that if she retired and was home all day, she would invest in caring for her mother.

Scan through the text and list five things that Grace thought about doing with her mother. (Page 201)

(a) She would serve her healthy meals.

(b) She would oversee her medication.

(c) She would take her for walks and to the park.

(d) She would take her to church.

(e) She would take her to get her hair done as well as manicures and pedicures.

Character Trait Discussion

The Character Trait for Lesson Three is "acceptance".
Acceptance means to leave something the way it is and not try to change it.

Read the statement below. Then choose one of the questions below and answer it. Write your answer in the space provided then discuss it with your group.

Grace accepts that because of her mother's condition, she cannot have a normal relationship with her.

1. Would you accept someone the way they are, or would you expect them to change? Explain.

2. Do you think it is important to accept others with their flaws? Why or why not?

3. How would you react if your friend was making fun of someone with a disability?

_____**Answers will vary from learner to learner.**_____

_____

_____

_____

_____

_____

Lesson Four - Answers

This lesson coincides with a diary entry dated August 22, 2018 from "Diary of Emotions: Thoughts and Feelings". The purpose of this lesson is to uncover important details to understand the situation of the characters.
Entry Date: August 22, 2018

Main Idea and Supporting Details
Place an "X" on the line beside the "main idea" of the story.

___X___ Grace is eager to know more details about her mother's life.

_____ Grace feels bad for her mother not being able to have her family.

_____ Grace has a lot of admiration for her grandmother.

The <u>four</u> statements below "support" the main idea. Fill in the blanks with the correct word.

(a) From this entry, we learn that Grace's mother was adopted when she was **two** years old. (Page 208)

(b) Grace's mother was skilled at playing the **piano**. (Page 209)

(c) Grace's mother seemed **nonchalant** and did not worry about her relationship with her husband. (Page 210)

(d) Grace felt **disappointed** in her father for putting his wife in a mental hospital and not visiting her. (Page 210)

Literary Elements: Theme
In any literary work, the theme is the underlying message that the writer would like to get across. Circle all the themes that you can find in this diary entry. (Page 210)

(a) **betrayal**
(b) individual vs. society
(c) **love and sacrifice**
(d) **motherhood**
(e) loss of innocence
(f) role of women

Literary Techniques

A literary technique is any method that the author uses to convey their message. Literary techniques are different from literary elements.

The following are some literary techniques:

Backstory: *This is a story that precedes the events in the story being told. This is some background information that adds meaning to current circumstances.*

Cliffhanger: *The story ends unsolved in order to interest the audience in a future episode for the resolution.*

Foreshadowing: *The author uses this technique to suggest events, which are yet to happen in the story.*

Look at the example from the diary entry and decide which literary technique the author has employed to convey her message.

"Now it all makes sense. I believe my grandmother did what she had to do in the situation. She could not have children of her own. She saw this cute little neglected girl, and took the steps necessary to have this little girl so she could take care of her."

(a) Backstory

(b) Cliffhanger

(c) Foreshadowing

Identifying Cause and Effect

"Finding her has just put a completely different view on the situation. I have peace, contentment, and comfort; and I feel empowered."

What is the Cause? <u>Finding her has just put a completely different view on the situation.</u>

What is the Effect? <u>I have peace, contertment, and comfort; and I feel empowered.</u>

Reading for Information
Scan through the entry to find the answers for the following questions:

How many years was Grace's mother married after she left Kansas City? (Page 207)   **Two**

Name one or more things that Grandmother taught Grace's mother. (Page 208)
playing the piano/talking with correct grammar/ dressing nicely/proper etiquette

Character Trait Discussion
The Character Trait for Lesson Four is "curiosity".
Curiosity means a strong desire to know or learn something.

Read the statement below. Then choose <u>one</u> of the questions below and answer it. Write your answer in the space provided then discuss it with your group.

In this entry, we see Grace's thirst for information, as she wants to know more about her mother's youth and marriage to her father.

1. What is something you are curious about and why?

2. Do you think it is good to be curious? Why or why not?

3. What would you do if you could not get the information you needed?

_____**Answers will vary from learner to learner.**_____

Lesson Five

This lesson coincides with a diary entry dated September 9, 2018 from "Diary of Emotions: Thoughts and Feelings". The purpose of this lesson is to understand the cause of the characters' feelings towards each other.
Entry Date: September 9, 2018

Main Idea and Supporting Details
Place an "X" on the line beside the "main idea" of the story.

_____ Grace hates to admit that her father was right about her mother.

__X__ Grace is now okay with her mother not being in her life.

_____ Grace's mother just did not want any children.

The <u>four</u> statements below "support" the main idea. Fill in the blanks with the correct word.

(Page 212)

(a) Grace's mother did not **receive** her and her siblings when they got to her.

(b) She seems to be **satisfied** without being in contact with Grace and her siblings.

(c) Grace feels **emotional** about her mother being okay without her.

(d) Grace believes that her mother left for a **reason**.

Literary Elements: Tone
The tone is the attitude of the author towards a subject or an audience.
Based on the lines below, decide on the tone for this entry.

"In all actuality, I pretty much feel the same way. Even though I am feeling emotional about this, there is still that part of me that feels like she has not been in my life for all of these years, so I am perfectly okay with her not being in my life now."

(a) amused

(b) resentful

(c) pragmatic

Identifying Cause and Effect

"So, I am in my feelings about the last time I called my mother and she said she did not feel like talking to anybody. This brings back memories of how my father would tell us that my mother probably would not receive us if we ever found her."

What is the Cause? <u>This brings back memories of how my father would tell us that my mother probably would not receive us if we ever found her.</u>

What is the Effect? <u>I am in my feelings about the last time I called my mother and she said she did not feel like talking to anybody.</u>

Interpreting and Evaluating Information

Based on your reading of the text, do you think Grace is still holding a grudge against her mother for abandoning her children? Explain your answer.

Sample answer: <u>No, she does not seem to hold a grudge against her mother. Instead, she seems to have accepted that her mother is satisfied with being on her own. Although it emotionally affects her a little, Grace is okay with not having her mother in her life, since she was not there for the so many years anyway.</u>

Character Trait Discussion
The Character Trait for Lesson Five is "adaptable".
Adaptable means being able to adjust to new conditions.

Read the statement below. Then choose <u>one</u> of the questions below and answer it. Write your answer in the space provided then discuss it with your group.

Grace shows adaptability in being okay with her mother not wanting to be with her.

1. Describe a situation where being adaptable will be advantageous to you.

2. Do you think being adaptable to new situations give you a better outlook in life?

   Explain why or why not?

3. Do you think change is good or bad? Discuss.

_____**Answers will vary from learner to learner.**_____

Lesson Six - Answers

This lesson coincides with a diary entry dated September 12, 2018 from "Diary of Emotions: Thoughts and Feelings". The purpose of this lesson is to understand observe some key events in the story to understand characters better.
Entry Date: September 12, 2018

Main Idea and Supporting Details
Place an "X" on the line beside the "main idea" of the story.

_____ Grace is thinking about furnishing her mother's room and buying her a phone.

__**X**__ Grace's mother does not remember the memories that Grace shares with her.

_____ Grace is appreciative of her father for trying to keep the family together.

The <u>four</u> statements below "support" the main idea. Fill in the blanks with the correct word.

(a) Grace's mother volunteered in the **children's nursery** at the church they used to go to. (Page 213)

(b) She did not remember buying Grace **malt balls candy** at the store. (Page 213)

(c) When she was a child, Grace would get into her mother's closet and put on her **clothes** and **shoes**. (Page 215)

(d) She **denied** being beaten by her husband and claimed that he treated her well. (Page 215)

Literary Elements: Style
In literature, style refers to the way the author uses words. It can include word choice, sentence structure, figurative language, mood, images and tone.

Here are some examples of styles in literature:

Expository: This is mainly used for facts, educational information and is sometimes instructional in nature.

Descriptive: This style of writing includes a lot of descriptions. The author will use adjectives, adverbs, metaphors and sometimes poetic language to express their thoughts.

Persuasive: This style of writing targets a specific audience to persuade them towards a certain point of view. It presents an argument by presenting evidence to support an opinion.

What style does the author employ for these diary entries?

(a) Expository

(b) Descriptive

(c) Persuasive

Identifying Cause and Effect

"I told her I remembered her laying in the grass in the backyard crying, afraid of being taken away. She did not really respond to that. Probably because it was a hurtful moment, and she preferred to talk about things that felt good to her."

What is the Cause? <u>I told her I remembered her laying in the grass in the backyard crying, afraid of being taken away.</u>

What is the Effect? <u>She did not really respond to that. Probably because it was a hurtful moment, and she preferred to talk about things that felt good to her.</u>

Interpreting and Evaluating Information

Does the author feel more appreciative of her father in this entry?

Please expound on your answer.

Sample answer: <u>Yes, the author feels more appreciative of her father in this entry as she remembers her birth certificate showing him taking her home from the hospital when she was born. She even says it was "honorable" of him to do that. At first, she does not approve of her father beating her mother, but she realizes that he was trying to protect them. Grace believes that her father tried to keep the family together and really did care about her and her siblings.</u>

Character Trait Discussion

The Character Trait for Lesson Six is "compassionate".
Compassionate means showing sympathy and concern for others.

Read the statement below. Then choose one of the questions below and answer it. Write your answer in the space provided then discuss it with your group.

Throughout the story, we have seen how compassionate Grace is with her mother despite the unexpected outcome. She even plans to provide a comfortable life for her mother.

1. Describe one instance where you were compassionate towards someone.

2. Do you think being compassionate all the time is a weakness? Discuss.

3. How would you deal with someone who treats people badly?

_____**Answers will vary from learner to learner**_____

_____

_____

_____

_____

_____

_____

_____

_____

_____

_____

_____

_____

Lesson Seven - Answers

> This lesson coincides with a diary entry dated September 15, 2018 from "Diary of Emotions: Thoughts and Feelings". The purpose of this lesson is elucidate lines from the text and analyze the emotions of the main character.
> **Entry Date:** September 15, 2018

Main Idea and Supporting Details

Place an "X" on the line beside the "main idea" of the story.

___X___ Grace has come to a realization that her mother actually does not want her.

_____ Grace's mother did not come to the phone because her hip was hurting.

_____ Grace only called her mother to check if she had received a package.

The <u>four</u> statements below "support" the main idea. Fill in the blanks with the correct word.

(a) Grace wondered if her mother was using her hip pain as an **excuse** to avoid coming to the phone. (Page 217)

(b) Grace feels almost temped to **give up** trying to have an ongoing relationship with her mother. (Page 218)

(c) Grace's **father** and **grandmother** told her that her mother did not want her. (Page 218)

(d) She finally accepts that they were telling the **truth** about her mother. (Page 218)

Author's Purpose

Circle the letter for the correct answer.

What is the author trying to do for the reader in this diary entry?

(a) The author wants to <u>inform</u> the reader by teaching something.

(b) The author wants to <u>entertain</u> the reader by using something amusing.

(c) The author wants to <u>persuade</u> the reader to believe her point of view.

(d) The author wants to <u>create a mood</u> with descriptions to stir emotions in the reader.

Identifying Cause and Effect

"April said she would be sure to have her to call me tomorrow. We will see. Otherwise, I am almost tempted to give up trying to have an ongoing relationship with her."

What is the Cause? <u>April said she would be sure to have her to call me tomorrow. We will see.</u>

What is the Effect? <u>Otherwise, I am almost tempted to give up trying to have an ongoing relationship with her.</u>

Interpreting and Evaluating Information
What is the tone of the author in the following lines from the entry?

"I know she doesn't dislike me. She just never wanted so many children, and since she has been on her own for so long, she is happier that way."

(a) bitter

(b) benevolent

(c) aggrieved

(d) concerned

Character Trait Discussion
The Character Trait for Lesson Seven is "generous".
Generous means showing a readiness to give more of something.

Read the statement below. Then choose <u>one</u> of the questions below and answer it. Write your answer in the space provided then discuss it with your group.

Grace has shown generosity towards her mother in terms of affection and material things. In this entry, Grace calls the boarding home to check with her mother if she received something she sent her.

1. Name someone who you think is very generous and explain why.

2. How would being generous be advantageous to a person?

3. Describe any generous act that you did for someone.

_____**Answers will vary from learner to learner.**_____

Lesson Eight - Answers

This lesson coincides with a diary entry dated September 16, 2018 from "Diary of Emotions: Thoughts and Feelings". The purpose of this lesson is to be able to empathize with the main character and understand her conflict.
Entry Date: September 16, 2018

Main Idea and Supporting Details
Place an "X" on the line beside the "main idea" of the story.

_____ Grace is upset with her mother for not calling her about the package.

__X__ Grace is having mixed feelings about continuing to keep in touch with her mother.

_____ Grace does not want to buy her mother more things because they could be stolen.

The <u>four</u> statements below "support" the main idea. Fill in the blanks with the correct word.

(a) Grace is considering not calling her mother again since she does not seem **interested**. (Page 220)

(b) Grace's mother said that she was in the hospital because she wanted a **break** from all of her children. (Page 220)

(c) Grace feels that she should simply be **happy** with having found her mother before she passed away. (Page 222)

(d) Grace's mother has been living in a boarding home for **fifteen** years. (Page 222)

Literary Elements: Conflict
Read the following lines from the entry and decide what sort of conflict Grace is battling.

"Well anyway, I have a decision to make. I have to decide if I am going to continue to try to reach out to her when it seems as if she does not really care about that. I feel torn between continuing to call her and stopping calling her. I guess I could talk to April about it first. April would probably say, "Just keep calling her," because she needs family even if she does not act as if she does."

(a) Person vs. Person   **(b) Person vs. Self**   (c) Person vs. Fate

Identifying Cause and Effect

"That could also be why neither he, nor my grandmother, took us to visit her in the mental hospital leading up to her disappearance. My father seemed to have known she would not receive us, so taking us to see her might have been more harmful for us than helpful."

What is the Cause? <u>My father seemed to have known she would not receive us.</u>

What is the Effect? <u>That could also be why neither he, nor my grandmother, took us to visit her in the mental hospital leading up to her disappearance.</u>

Reading for Information
Scan through the entry to find the answers for the following questions. Answer them in a word or two. (Page 221)

(a) What desire did Geneva talk about during the therapy session?   **knitting**

(b) What is the name of Grace's daughter?   **Arica**

Interpreting and Evaluating Information
Read the following sentence and answer the question that follows.

"I guess my choice would be to know her, but I realize I am not going to have a mother in the way that I would like to."

Why do you think Grace prefers to know her mother despite the way she is?

(a) She does not want to enjoy the experience of having a mother.
(b) She spent so many years searching for her mother and wanting to know her.
(c) She wants to be able to take care of her and win her affection.

Character Trait Discussion
The Character Trait for Lesson Eight is "sensible".
Sensible means being practical and reasonable.

Read the statement below. Then choose <u>one</u> of the questions below and answer it. Write your answer in the space provided then discuss it with your group.

In this entry, Grace is sensible in analyzing her mother's condition and possible reasons for not talking to her. She even considers not sending her things because it would make her a target for the people living in the boarding home.

1. Do you think being sensible is better than being generous? Discuss with relevant examples.

2. Would you consider yourself a sensible decision maker? Explain why or why not.

3. Would you prefer to win a lot of money or go on vacation to a dream destination? Explain.

_____Answers will vary from learner to learner._____

Lesson Nine - Answers

This lesson coincides with a diary entry dated September 17, 2018 from "Diary of Emotions: Thoughts and Feelings". The purpose of this lesson is to understand the role of supporting characters in influencing the main conflict of the story.
Entry Date: September 17, 2018

Main Idea and Supporting Details
Place an "X" on the line beside the "main idea" of the story.

_____ Grace's father did not understand that her mother had a serious mental illness.

_____ Grace's sister has the exact same mental illness that her mother suffers from.

___X___ **Grace finally understands the struggles that her father underwent with her mother.**

The <u>four</u> statements below "support" the main idea. Fill in the blanks with the correct word.

(a) Grace remembers that her father was **protective** over her and her siblings. (Page 224)

(b) Grace realizes the **hardships** her father experienced just to keep the family together. (Page 224)

(c) Grace's father had gone through a lot trying to **raise six** children. (Page 225)

(d) Grace thought her father was making **excuses** when he was talking badly about her mother. (Page 225)

Making Inferences
Read the following line from the entry and answer the question.

"I never fully understood his anger and I never fully understood my father's commitment to us until I met and talked to my mother."

Why did it take so long for Grace to understand her father's commitment?

(a) She needed enough evidence from her siblings to prove that her father cared.

(b) She just needed time to think and analyze her father because she was too young.

(c) She needed to know her mother's side of the story before believing what her father said.

Character Analysis

Write 2 positive and 2 negative things about Grace's father in the table below. (Page 224-226)

Grace's Father	
Positives	**Negatives**
1. He was very protective of Grace and her siblings, and cared about them. 2. He always took Grace's side even if she did something wrong.	1. He would beat his wife. 2. He did not tell Grace's sister that she had a mental illness and get her treated.

Identifying Cause and Effect

"It really made me feel some kind of a way that this worker knew my mother would be happy to see her son."

What is the Cause? this worker knew my mother would be happy to see her son.

What is the Effect? It really made me feel some kind of a way

Character Trait Discussion
The Character Trait for Lesson Nine is "unprejudiced".
Unprejudiced means not having or showing unfair bias or prejudice.
Read the statement below. Then choose one of the questions below and answer it. Write your answer in the space provided then discuss it with your group.
Grace is unprejudiced when thinking about both her parents. She tries to understand the struggle faced by both of them, rather than judging quickly.

1. Do you think is it good to be unprejudiced in life? Why or why not?

2. Are you quick to judge people? How can you tell if someone is a nice person?

3. How would you deal with someone who misunderstood you and blamed you for something?

_____Answers will vary from learner to learner._____

Lesson Ten - Answers

This lesson coincides with a diary entry dated September 30, 2018 from "Diary of Emotions: Thoughts and Feelings". The purpose of this lesson is to uncover more details about a specific character to understand them better.
Entry Date: September 30, 2018

Main Idea and Supporting Details
Place an "X" on the line beside the "main idea" of the story

_____ Grace appreciates her brother Jerome for sharing more details about her mother.

__X__ **Grace's mother, Geneva was skilled at doing things other than playing the piano.**

_____ Grace's wants to move Geneva to Kansas City to buy her all of her favorite things.

The four statements below "support" the main idea. Fill in the blanks with the correct word. (Page 230)

(a) Geneva was good at doing things whenever she took her **medication** properly.

(b) **Jerome** and **Grandmother** told Grace about how talented her mother was.

(c) Jerome said that their mother's **cooking** was homemade and delicious.

(d) Grace wants to buy Geneva a **piano** and a **sewing machine** if she moves to Kansas.

Reading for Information
Scan through the text and list all the things that Geneva was good at doing. (Page 230)

1. **sewing**

2. **knitting**

3. **cooking**

4. **playing the piano**

Would Geneva still have all of her special talents today? (Page 230)

(a) Yes   (b) No

Identifying Cause and Effect

"Knowing those things that she is good at makes me want to bring her to Kansas City and get her involved in those things that she loves…"

What is the Cause? <u>Knowing those things that she is good at</u>

What is the Effect? <u>makes me want to bring her to Kansas City and get her involved in those things that she loves…</u>

Character Trait Discussion
The Character Trait for Lesson Ten is "talented".
Talented means having a natural aptitude or skill for something.

Read the statement below. Then choose <u>one</u> of the questions below and answer it. Write your answer in the space provided then discuss it with your group.

In this entry, we discover that Geneva had other talents besides playing the piano.

1. Name two or more of your talents? When did you discover you had them?

2. Have you ever made use of your talents to help someone? Explain how.

3. Describe an activity that you enjoy doing alone.

_____**Answers will vary from learner to learner.**_____

_____

_____

_____

_____

_____

_____

_____

Lesson Eleven - Answers

> This lesson coincides with a diary entry dated October 5, 2018 from "Diary of Emotions: Thoughts and Feelings". The purpose of this lesson is to identify the dilemma of the main character.
> **Entry Date:** October 5, 2018

Main Idea and Supporting Details

Place an "X" on the line beside the "main idea" of the story.

_____ Grace wishes that she could have a normal relationship with her mother.

___X__ **Grace's accepts that her mother has a mental illness, but feels deprived of a relationship with her.**

_____ Grace is happy she found her mother even if she has a mental illness.

The two *statements below "support" the main idea. Fill in the blanks with the correct word.*

(a) Grace tells us what it is like to be related to someone with a **mental illness**. (Page 231)

(b) She also says that accepting them like that does not take way the **pain** of

not having a normal relationship with them. (Page 231)

Making Inferences

"Sometimes, I wonder what is harder: living without a mother and not knowing her, or knowing her and having to live with the reality of her mental illness."

How do you think Grace is feeling about her mother in the lines above?

Sample answer: Grace is confused about the status of her current relationship with her mother. She does not know how to feel about it since her mother is mentally ill and not capable of being the parent she expects her to be. However, Grace wonders if living without a mother and never knowing her is harder than knowing her and living with the reality of her mental illness. Although she is content with the latter, she still experiences feelings of frustration and rejection from time to time.

Character Trait Discussion
The Character Trait for Lesson Eleven is "perceptive".
Perceptive means having or showing sensitive insight.

Read the statement below. Then choose one of the questions below and answer it. Write your answer in the space provided then discuss it with your group.

In this entry, Grace is perceptive about the reality of being related to someone with a mental illness.

1. Do you consider yourself a perceptive person? Explain why or why not.

2. Do you know someone who is perceptive? If so, who? Please explain.

3. Do you think that being perceptive important? Why or why not?

_____**Answers will vary from learner to learner.**_____

_____

_____

_____

_____

_____

_____

_____

_____

_____

_____

_____

_____

Lesson Twelve - Answers

This lesson coincides with a diary entry dated October 6, 2018 from "Diary of Emotions: Thoughts and Feelings". The purpose of this lesson is to understand the emotional impact of the situation on the main character.
Entry Date: October 6, 2018

Main Idea and Supporting Details
Place an "X" on the line beside the "main idea" of the story.

___X___ Grace feels unwanted by her mother despite finding her after all these years.

_____ Grace's father left Grace and siblings alone while he worked in Florida.

_____ Grace is grateful to that she finally found her mother and can do things for her.

The four statements below "support" the main idea. Fill in the blanks with the correct word.

(a) Grace feels **disappointed** and **heartbroken** even though she found her mother. (Page 233)

(b) Geneva's story about why she didn't take her children with her, was **nothing** like how Grace expected it to be. (Page 233)

(c) Grace is disappointed with Geneva since she did not keep her **promise** of calling her the next day. (Page 234)

(d) Grace is considering if it would be best to simply **back away** from her mother. (Page 235)

Making Inferences

"I am happy to know she is in a stable place where she has been long-term, and she is not living on the streets. I can rest in the fact that this situation is the best it can be."

How does Grace feel about the situation with her mother in the lines above?

(a) She is happy that she has found her mother and need not care after this.
(b) She wants to accept that her mother is happy and lives in a stable place.
(c) She does not want to pressure her mother into moving to Kansas City.

Identifying Cause and Effect

"I believe it may have still been hard not having her at home. I would have likely felt responsible for her, starting at a very young age."

What is the Cause? <u>I believe it may have still been hard not having her at home.</u>

What is the Effect? <u>I would have likely felt responsible for her, starting at a very young age.</u>

Character Decisions and Actions

There are many things in a story that can influence a character to take an action.

Even though Grace knows her mother does not want her, why does she continue to care for her mother?

Sample answer: <u>Grace feels obligated to take care of her mother since she has finally found her after almost fifty years. She is aware of her mother's mental illness and knows that her mother is not capable of doing anything for her. However, finding and caring for her mother is something she has been dreaming of doing for a long time. So she puts her own emotions on the burn burner when dealing with her mother. Sometimes she feels tempted to back away and not continue to have a relationship with her mother because of the disinterested signals she receives from her. But she does care about her mother and hopes that she would want to move to Kansas City to be near her.</u>

Character Trait Discussion
The Character Trait for Lesson Twelve is "dutiful".
Dutiful means obediently fulfilling one's duty.
Read the statement below. Then choose <u>one</u> of the questions below and answer it. Write your answer in the space provided then discuss it with your group.
Grace is dutiful in the sense that she continues to fulfil the duties of a daughter to her mother.

1. Describe a situation where you were obligated to do something for someone.
2. What happens if you do not do something you are supposed to do?
3. Do you think it is better to be dutiful or not have responsibilities? Explain.

_____**Answers will vary from learner to learner.**_____

_____

Lesson Thirteen - Answers

> This lesson coincides with a diary entry dated October 8, 2018 from "Diary of Emotions: Thoughts and Feelings". The purpose of this lesson is to understand how the author copes with her situation.
> **Entry Date:** October 8, 2018

Main Idea and Supporting Details

Place an "X" on the line beside the "main idea" of the story.

_____ Grace put all of her feelings about her mother into heartfelt poems and songs.

_____ Grace believes she has no reason to cry except for how unfortunate the situation is.

__X__ Grace believes there is no reason to cry since her mother is taking care of herself.

The four statements below "support" the main idea. Fill in the blanks with the correct word. (Page 236)

(a) Grace thought that she would find her mother safe and secure in a **mental hospital**.

(b) Grace feels that her mother is probably **stronger** than her.

(c) Grace is happy that her mother does not walk the **streets** anymore.

(d) Grace now knows that her mother is strong enough to **take care** of herself.

Reading for Information

Scan the text and find the answer for the following question.

According to the author's observations, what are Geneva's daily activities? (Page 236)

1. **smoking cigarettes**

2. **eating breakfast, lunch and dinner**

3. **going to bed**

4. **getting up**

5. **going to the center**

6. **talking to people**

Identifying Cause and Effect

"She has been out there. She knows the streets. She was robbed on the streets. Now, she is afraid and I feel sad about that."

What is the Cause? <u>She has been out there. She knows the streets. She was robbed on the streets.</u>
What is the Effect? <u>Now, she is afraid and I feel sad about that.</u>

Interpreting and Evaluating Information

What do you think motivated Geneva to learn to take care of herself?

Sample answer: <u>Geneva used to look to her husband (Grace's father) for support and care since she has a mental illness. After she left the family, she had married a man named Calvin whom she thought would take care of her. She then ended up on the streets and had to fend for herself. It is during this time that she got robbed and lost everything. Being alone and having nobody to care for her probably taught her to take care of herself, and that is how she could have ended up in the boarding home. Grace also states that her mother is a strong woman.</u>

Character Trait Discussion
The Character Trait for Lesson Thirteen is "magnanimous".
Magnanimous means to be generous or forgiving.

Read the statement below. Then choose <u>one</u> of the questions below and answer it. Write your answer in the space provided then discuss it with your group.

Grace is magnanimous to her mother by understanding her struggle and caring for her. She has also forgiven her mother for leaving her so many years ago.

1. Describe how someone has been magnanimous to you.

2. Is it easy for you to forgive a person who did you wrong? Explain why or why not.

3. Would you forgive someone for what they did even if they do not change? Discuss.

_____**Answers will vary from learner to learner.**_____

Lesson Fourteen - Answers

> This lesson coincides with a diary entry dated October 26, 2018 from "Diary of Emotions: Thoughts and Feelings". The purpose of this lesson is to observe the similarities the author has with her mother.
> **Entry Date:** October 26, 2018

Main Idea and Supporting Details
Place an "X" on the line beside the "main idea" of the story.

_____ Grace cannot remember from whom she picked up certain traits and mannerisms.

_____ Grace's oldest sister Carla had picked up many things from their mother.

___X__ Grace believes that she and her mother share some similarities.

The four statements below "support" the main idea. Fill in the blanks with the correct word.
(Page 237)

(a) Grace has some **characteristics** that are similar to her mother.

(b) They both say **"Oh, Wow!"** in the exact same way.

(c) Grace has always said those words and so does her **daughter**.

(d) **Carla** had probably picked up the saying from their mother as she was 8 years old.

Interpreting and Evaluating Information
Read the excerpt below and discuss the following two questions.

"Our "Oh, wow!" Is probably not hereditary. It is probably environmental."

How do you think Grace learned the saying "Oh, Wow!" when her mother was not around? What is the difference between hereditary inheritance and environmental inheritance?

Sample answer: Grace is guessing that she could have picked it up from her sister, Carla who had been 8 years old at the time their mother left. Carla would say "Oh, Wow!" in the exact way their mother did, and Grace probably picked it up from her. Grace knows that saying these words in the exact way as her mother is not hereditary, as it wasn't passed down to her through birth. She instead learned it from the environment she grew up in i.e. through copying Carla.

Character Trait Discussion

The Character Trait for Lesson Fourteen is "introspective".
The word **"introspective"** refers to someone who spends a lot of time examining their own thoughts and feelings.

Read the statement below. Then choose <u>one</u> of the questions below and answer it. Write your answer in the space provided then discuss it with your group.

Through this diary entry, the author is examining herself as to where and how she acquired certain characteristics. She is being introspective by analyzing her own traits and feelings.

1. Do you have a specific trait or mannerism that you inherited from someone? Discuss.

2. If you could change something about yourself, what would it be and why?

3. Do you think it is good to indulge in self-examination and exploration? Why or why not?

_____**Answers will vary from learner to learner.**_____

Lesson Fifteen - Answers

> This lesson coincides with a diary entry dated November 1, 2018 from "Diary of Emotions: Thoughts and Feelings". The purpose of this lesson is to understand the reason for the author not going ahead with a plan.
> **Entry Date:** November 1, 2018

Main Idea and Supporting Details
Place an "X" on the line beside the "main idea" of the story.

_____ Grace thinks it is important for her son, nieces and nephews to meet Geneva.

__X__ Grace has thought many times about having her mother live with her.

_____ Grace is thinking about what could have happened if the wrong Geneva had come to the phone instead.

The <u>four</u> statements below "support" the main idea. Fill in the blanks with the correct word. (Pages 238-239)

(a) At first, Grace thought that she would bring Geneva home so that all of her **grandchildren** would be able to meet her.

(b) The thought of moving to where Geneva lives, was only a **passing** thought for Grace.

(c) Since Grace does not know Geneva too well, it would likely not be a good **decision** for her to live with her.

(d) Grace does not see Geneva moving to where she lives as a real **possibility**.

Making Inferences
Circle all of the reasons that Grace states for deciding not to have her mother live with her.

(a) She has given up on her mother being in her life.
(b) The boarding home takes care of all of Geneva's basic needs.
(c) Grace is still holding a grudge against Geneva for abandoning her.
(d) Geneva has been on her own for a very long time.
(e) Caring for Geneva may be a challenge since Grace does not know what her medical needs are.

Reading for Information

How did Grace know what Geneva sounded like when they spoke on the phone for the first time in years? (Page 238)

(a) She had always imagined what she would sound like for years.

(b) Her siblings had given her vivid descriptions of what she used to sound like.

(c) Her father would mock her mother's voice and she was able to recognize it on the phone.

(d) She had a recording of her mother's voice from a long time ago.

Identifying Cause and Effect

"She has been on her own for a very long time and, actually, so have I. It would probably be uncomfortable for us both."

What is the Cause? She has been on her own for a very long time and, actually, so have I.

What is the Effect? It would probably be uncomfortable for us both.

Character Trait Discussion
The Character Trait for Lesson Fifteen is "rational".
Rational means basing an idea on clear thought and reason.

Read the statement below. Then choose one of the questions below and answer it. Write your answer in the space provided then discuss it with your group.

Grace is being rational in considering both the good and bad of having her mother live with her. It is only after careful analysis of the situation that she decides it is better her mother stays where she is.

1. What would happen if you let your emotions get in the way of rational decision-making?

2. Would you consider yourself a rational person? Explain why or why not.

3. Do you think rational thinking important in order to get through a difficult situation? Why or why not?

_____Answers will vary from learner to learner._____

_____

Lesson Sixteen - Answers

This lesson coincides with a diary entry dated November 20, 2018 from "Diary of Emotions: Thoughts and Feelings". The purpose of this lesson is to observe the difference in character decisions.
Entry Date: November 20, 2013

Main Idea and Supporting Details
Place an "X" on the line beside the "main idea" of the story.

_____ Geneva left on her own accord and not because of how her husband treated her.
_____ Grace's intention was to spend every moment with Geneva while they were visiting.
___X___ **Grace is thinking about the time she and her brothers went to reunite with Geneva.**

The four statements below "support" the main idea. Fill in the blanks with the correct word. (Page 240)

(a) Grace and her brothers went back the next day to have a **chicken** dinner with Geneva.

(b) **Jerome** declined the opportunity to go back.

(c) Grace intended to try to bring her mother home and build a **relationship** with her.

(d) Grace and Jerome had **different** intentions for their mother.

Character Decisions and Action
Grace and her older brother Jerome had different intentions when they reunited with their mother. Mention what they wanted to do in the table below.

Grace	Jerome
Grace thought about spending every moment with her mother while they were there, and getting her to go back with them to build a relationship with her.	Jerome did not want to go back for dinner with Geneva the next day. He just wanted to see her, enjoy her, take a few pictures with her and share the wonderful memory with his family.

Character Trait Discussion
The Character Trait for Lesson Sixteen is "optimistic".
Optimistic means being hopeful and confident about the future.

Read the statement below. Then choose <u>one</u> of the questions below and answer it. Write your answer in the space provided then discuss it with your group.

In the story, we saw that Grace had been optimistic about reuniting with her mother and having her live with her in Kansas.

1. Does being optimistic always lead to a positive outcome? Discuss.

2. What are some things you are optimistic about, and why?

3. Why is the difference between and "optimistic" and an "opportunistic" person?

_____**Answers will vary from learner to learner.**_____

_____

_____

_____

_____

_____

_____

_____

_____

_____

_____

Lesson Seventeen - Answers

This lesson coincides with a diary entry dated November 22, 2018 from "Diary of Emotions: Thoughts and Feelings". The purpose of this lesson is to analyze the author's feeling about the kind of relationship she has with her mother.
Entry Date: November 22, 2018

Main Idea and Supporting Details
Place an "X" on the line beside the "main idea" of the story.

_____ Geneva confirmed that she had received the package that Grace sent her.
_____ Geneva wanted more yarn in order to knit a large men's sweater.
__**X**__ After calling her mother, Grace had mixed feelings about sending her more things.

The four statements below "support" the main idea. Fill in the blanks with the correct word.
(Page 241)

(a) Geneva liked the **yarn** and **knitting needles** that Grace had sent her.

(b) Grace felt **disappointed** that someone had stolen the cod liver oil she sent Geneva.

(c) After the phone call, Grace ended up sending her some **instruction books**.

(d) Grace also felt **guilty** for not sending Geneva the additional yarn she wanted.

Making Inferences
Read the following line from the entry and answer the question.

"Thoughts of, "she should be living here with us," came to my mind. However, I know she is happy there. The thought of never sending anything there again also came to my mind."

Why do you think Grace was experiencing mixed feelings in this situation?

(a) Geneva had taken so long to confirm that she had received the package.

(b) Someone had stolen the cod liver oil that Grace sent for Geneva.

(c) She said that she needed more yarn for knitting a garment.

(d) There was no proof that Geneva was even using the things Grace was sending her.

Reading for Information

What are the two reasons for which Geneva had not begun using the knitting kit that Grace had sent her?

1. **She did not have any instruction books on how to get started.**

2. **She needed more yarn to knit a large men's sweater.**

Character Trait Discussion
The Character Trait for Lesson Seventeen is "practical".
Practical means fitting the needs of a particular situation in a helpful way.

Read the statement below. Then choose <u>one</u> of the questions below and answer it. Write your answer in the space provided then discuss it with your group.

In this chapter, Grace is practical in not sending her mother the extra yarn that she needed because it might be stolen, or just not be used. By doing this, she is also lessening the burden for her mother in having to keep valuable things safe.

1. What other practical solution would you offer the author in this situation?

2. Do you think being practical can lead to misunderstandings in certain situations? Should that stop you from being practical?

3. Are you a practical person? Write three reasons to support your claim.

_____**Answers will vary from learner to learner.**_____

_____

_____

_____

_____

_____

_____

Lesson Eighteen - Answers

This lesson coincides with a diary entry dated December 1, 2018 from "Diary of Emotions: Thoughts and Feelings". The purpose of this lesson is to analyze the author's thoughts about some circumstances involving her mother.
Entry Date: December 1, 2018

Main Idea and Supporting Details
Place an "X" on the line beside the "main idea" of the story.

_____ Grace is thinking about moving Geneva to Kansas City soon.

_____ Grace is considering the possibility of them caring for Geneva when she can no longer take care of herself.

___X___ **Grace is not sure about what she would do if Geneva suddenly needed someone to take care of her.**

The three statements below "support" the main idea. Fill in the blanks with the correct word. (Page 242)

(a) Grace is wondering what she would do if the **boarding home** or **center** needed someone to care for Geneva.

(b) She is not sure if she should jump at the **opportunity** to bring her mother close to her.

(c) Grace believes that her mother's **mental illness** has controlled all of her decisions.

Making Inferences
Circle the letter for the correct statement.

How does Grace feel about when the time arrives for her mother to come live closer to her?

(a) She feels ready to take on the challenge of moving her mother to Kansas City.

(b) She is having mixed feelings and cannot tell what exactly she would do.

(c) She is thinking of how her mother might feel about living closer to them.

(d) She already has a plan for the time comes.

Character Trait Discussion
The Character Trait for Lesson Eighteen is "undecided".
Undecided means not having made a decision.

Read the statement below. Then choose one of the questions below and answer it. Write your answer in the space provided then discuss it with your group.

In this entry, Grace is undecided about what she would do when the time comes for someone to take care of her mother.

1. Describe a situation where you felt undecided about what you should do.

2. Do you think it is better to make decisions quickly in challenging situations or to take time?

3. Mention someone who is a good decision maker and explain why.

_____**Answers will vary from learner to learner.**_____

_____

_____

_____

_____

_____

_____

_____

_____

_____

_____

Lesson Nineteen - Answers

This lesson coincides with a diary entry dated January 23, 2019 from "Diary of Emotions: Thoughts and Feelings". The purpose of this lesson is to study the conversation and analyze character feelings.
Entry Date: January 23, 2019

Main Idea and Supporting Details
Place an "X" on the line beside the "main idea" of the story.

__X__ Grace called her mother after a few weeks had passed.
_____ Geneva informed Grace that she had received the box that she sent.
_____ Grace's grandmother always observed special occasions.

The <u>four</u> statements below "support" the main idea. Fill in the blanks with the correct word. (Page 243)

(a) When Grace called, Geneva came to the phone and was **happy** to hear from her.

(b) Geneva asked if Grace had spoken to **Carla** and **Terrence**.

(c) Geneva's hip felt better since she got a **shot** to help with the pain.

(d) Geneva reminded Grace that **Valentine's Day** was coming up.

Reading for Information
Scan the text and find the answers for the following questions. (Page 243)

1. How long had it been since Grace last called Geneva?   **four weeks or more**

2. When did Grace send the box to Geneva?   **before Christmas**

3. What did grandmother do for Grace at bedtime?   **bring her milkshakes**

Interpreting and Inferring

Read the following dialogue from the text and answer the question.

She said, "Thank you for calling. I like hearing your voice."
I said, "Thank you. I will try to call sooner next time."
She said, "Okay."

What can you tell about Geneva's feelings towards Grace based on her last response?
(Page 244)

(a) She is genuinely happy to hear from Grace and wants to know more about her life.

(b) She is looking forward to Grace calling her again soon.

(c) She didn't care when Grace would call again, but was happy that she called when she did.

Character Trait Discussion

The Character Trait for Lesson Nineteen is "responsible".
Responsible in this sense means having care for someone as a part of one's role.

Read the statement below. Then choose <u>one</u> of the questions below and answer it. Write your answer in the space provided then discuss it with your group.

Even though she has mixed feelings, Grace feels responsible for her mother and calls her occasionally to check on her.

1. What is one of your biggest responsibilities? How do you feel about it?

2. Is being responsible a duty or something done by choice?

3. Do you think it is wrong to shirk your responsibilities? Why or why not?

_____**Answers will vary from learner to learner.**_____

_____

_____

_____

_____

_____

Lesson Twenty - Answers

This lesson coincides with a diary entry dated April 20, 2019 from "Diary of Emotions: Thoughts and Feelings". The purpose of this lesson is to determine how characters will react to change.
Entry Date: April 20, 2019

Main Idea and Supporting Details
Place an "X" on the line beside the "main idea" of the story.

_____ Grace and her brothers showed Geneva a beautiful place to stay, but she declined.
__**X**__ **Geneva preferred to stay in the poor area where she is.**
_____ Grace and her brothers have decided to let Geneva stay where she is.

The four statements below "support" the main idea. Fill in the blanks with the correct word.
(Page 245)

(a) Geneva felt that Grace and her brothers were offering her **luxury** when

   Grace showed her the beautiful place.

(b) Grace feels that Geneva may not be **comfortable** living in a community that was

   not poor.

(c) Grace wonders if Geneva would still need to carry her **backpack** around even if

   she lived in a place where nobody would steal from her.

(d) Geneva is **content** to live at the boarding home because it is her home.

Reading for Information
Scan the text and find the answer for the following question.

Why are the problems faced by Geneva at the boarding home?

Sample answer: Geneva is surrounded by drugs every day and people who constantly steal from her. She is also afraid to walk around in the community for fear of harm. If she does not go get her food time, some other resident will eat it. She also has to carry around a backpack to protect all of her belongings.

Interpreting and Evaluating Information

Why does Geneva prefer to live at the boarding home and not close to Grace and her brothers? (Page 245)

(a) She is used to that way of life since she has been there for fifteen years.

(b) She knows the people there and they take care of her needs.

(c) She has been on her own for a long time and does not feel comfortable with her family.

(d) All of the above.

Character Trait Discussion
The Character Trait for Lesson Twenty is "self-reliant".
Self-reliant means being able to do things and make decisions by oneself.

Read the statement below. Then choose <u>one</u> of the questions below and answer it. Write your answer in the space provided then discuss it with your group.

Geneva is a self-reliant person, capable of taking care of herself. Since she has been on her own for long, she does not want to rely on someone else to provide for her entirely.

1. Do you think being self-reliant is better than depending on others for support? Discuss.
2. Is it good to be independent? How would an independent person solve their problems?
3. Are you a self-reliant person? Do others think you are? State your reasons.

_____**Answers will vary from learner to learner.**_____

_____

_____

_____

_____

_____

_____

Lesson Twenty-One - Answers

This lesson coincides with a diary entry dated April 20, 2019 from "Diary of Emotions: Thoughts and Feelings". The purpose of this lesson is to observe the author's decisions concerning her mother and determine if they are right or wrong.
Entry Date: April 20, 2019

Main Idea and Supporting Details

Place an "X" on the line beside the "main idea" of the story.

_____ Geneva has been getting strong medication for her hip problem.

_____ Geneva preferred another brand of cigarettes.

__X__ Grace feels guilty about sending her mother cigarettes.

The four statements below "support" the main idea. Fill in the blanks with the correct word.
(Page 246)

(a) Geneva told Grace that her favorite cigarettes were an **expensive** name brand cigarette.

(b) She said that she only smoked the affordable ones since she did not have **money** to buy the other brand.

(c) Grace does not feel comfortable sending her mother cigarettes because they are bad for her **health**.

(d) She found out that it was against the law to send **tobacco** through mail.

Character Decisions and Action

Although Grace feels guilty about sending cigarettes to her mother, she still considers it. Do you think she should have told her mother that it is bad for her, even if it was judgmental?

Sample answer: It would have probably been better if Grace had told her mother that cigarettes are bad for her health. However, Grace said that she does not know her mother too well, and saying that to her may offend her. She finds out that the law does not allow Tobacco to be sent though mail. She decides to send money instead. At this point, Grace is just trying to make her mother feel comfortable with her. She is letting her know that she can ask her for anything and she will provide it for her. Even though refusing to send her cigarettes is the right thing to do, it is not the right time for it.

(However, answers will vary from learner to learner.)
Write three things that Grace could send her mother instead of cigarettes.

Sample answers:

1. chocolates / candy
2. flowers / stuffed animals / clothing
3. money

Identifying Cause and Effect

"I decided I would just send money instead. However, there are challenges to sending money because she does not have any way of cashing a check or a money order."

What is the Cause? she does not have any way of cashing a check or a money order.

What is the Effect? I decided I would just send money instead.

Character Trait Discussion
The Character Trait for Lesson Twenty-One is "thoughtful".
Thoughtful means showing consideration for the needs of other people.

Read the statement below. Then choose <u>one</u> of the questions below and answer it. Write your answer in the space provided then discuss it with your group.

Grace has been very thoughtful in getting Geneva whatever she needs even if it is cigarettes.

1. What is the most thoughtful thing someone has done for you?
2. Describe something thoughtful that you did for someone.
3. Would you buy someone the things they wanted even if it was harmful for them? Why or why not?

_____Answers will vary from learner to learner._____

Lesson Twenty-Two - Answers

This lesson coincides with a diary entry dated April 28, 2019 from "Diary of Emotions: Thoughts and Feelings". The purpose of this lesson is to observe changes in the author's mother.
Entry Date: April 28, 2019

Main Idea and Supporting Details
Place an "X" on the line beside the "main idea" of the story.

_____ Grace had sent Geneva some money to buy herself cigarettes.
__**X**__ **Geneva called Grace on her own for the first time.**
_____ Grace has mixed feelings about Geneva calling her.

The four statements below "support" the main idea. Fill in the blanks with the correct word.
(Page 247)

(a) Geneva **initiated** a call to Grace even though she had not called her first.

(b) She had called Grace **two** times in a row.

(c) She called to inform Grace that she had not **received** the money yet.

(d) The boarding home workers did not **encourage** Geneva to make the call.

Making Predictions

Grace has mixed feelings in regard to Geneva calling her for the first time on her own. However, she only called to inform Grace that had not got the money she sent her.

Do you think Geneva is beginning to get more comfortable with Grace? Do you think she would eventually be dependent on Grace and finally agree to move to Kansas City? State your reasons.

Sample answer: Geneva felt motivated to call Grace because she wanted cigarettes and needed the money to buy it. Since the money had not arrived yet, she felt compelled to call even though the boarding home workers did not encourage her. This also could be a sign that Geneva is in fact getting more comfortable with Grace. Perhaps she considers Grace to be her provider. Geneva might not agree to move to Kansas City soon, but she might do it eventually if she feels like Grace can take care of all her needs.

(However, answers will vary from learner to learner.)

Character Trait Discussion
The Character Trait for Lesson Twenty-Two is "capable".
A **"capable"** person is someone who is able to do something effortlessly.

Read the statement below. Then choose <u>one</u> of the questions below and answer it. Write your answer in the space provided then discuss it with your group.
Grace never thought that Geneva was capable of initiating a phone call to her. Geneva has proved that she is capable of calling on her own too.

1. Name a few things that you can do effortlessly. Mention how long it took you to learn it.

2. Were you ever hesitant to try something new? Explain why.

3. How would a person find out if they are capable of doing something?

_____**Answers will vary from learner to learner.**_____

_____

_____

_____

_____

_____

_____

_____

_____

_____

_____

_____

_____

Lesson Twenty-Three - Answers

> This lesson coincides with a diary entry dated May 12, 2019 from "Diary of Emotions: Thoughts and Feelings". The purpose of this lesson is to determine how the author's mother feels about not receiving something from her.
> **Entry Date:** May 12, 2019

Main Idea and Supporting Details

Place an "X" on the line beside the "main idea" of the story.

___X___ Geneva did not receive the money sent by Grace at all.
_____ Grace has decided not to send her mother anything for a while.
_____ Nobody answered the phone when Grace called the boarding home.

The two statements below "support" the main idea. Fill in the blanks with the correct word. (Page 248)

(a) Grace feels **discouraged** because the money she sent never reached Geneva.

(b) She did not send a **Mother's Day card** for fear of it not reaching Geneva.

Making Predictions

How do you think Geneva is feeling since the money that Grace sent her never arrived?

Sample answer: Geneva is probably feeling like Grace did not send the money at all. She probably feels disappointed that she waited so long for the money and it did not arrive. She needed the money to buy her favorite brand of cigarettes. This could probably be the reason why it is difficult for Grace to get in touch with her on Mother's Day.

(However, answers will vary from learner to learner.)

Identifying Cause and Effect

"I am still feeling discouraged about the cash I sent last month never arriving, so I did not send a Mother's Day card for fear it would not reach her."

What is the Cause? Grace is feeling discouraged about the cash she sent never arriving.

What is the Effect? She did not send a Mother's Day card because she was worried that it would not arrive either.

Character Trait Discussion

The Character Trait for Lesson Twenty-Three is "giving".
Giving means to give something to someone voluntarily without expecting anything in return.

Read the statement below. Then choose <u>one</u> of the questions below and answer it. Write your answer in the space provided then discuss it with your group.

Grace has been very giving to her mother. She provides her mother with the things she wants even though she is not capable of doing anything for her.

1. Are you a giving person? Mention some nice things you have done.

2. It is better to be a giver or a receiver? Explain.

3. Describe something nice that someone has done for you.

_____**Answers will vary from learner to learner.**_____

Lesson Twenty-Four - Answers

This lesson coincides with a diary entry dated May 13, 2019 from "Diary of Emotions: Thoughts and Feelings". The purpose of this lesson is to observe the result of the author's action.
Entry Date: May 13, 2019

Main Idea and Supporting Details
Place an "X" on the line beside the "main idea" of the story.

_____ Grace called her mother because she did not want her to feel like she forgot Mother's Day.

_____ Grace decided that she was not going to send anything for a while.

__**X**__ **Grace did not hear from her mother anymore since the cash got lost in the mail.**

The <u>two</u> *statements below "support" the main idea. Fill in the blanks with the correct word.*

(Page 248)

(a) Geneva did not come to the **phone** when Grace called her on Mother's Day.

(b) A **worker** at the boarding home did not bother going and getting Geneva to talk to Grace.

Identifying Cause and Effect

"I have tried calling her since then, but she did not come to the phone. Therefore, after today, I may not be calling or sending anything for a while.

What is the Cause? I have tried calling her since then, but she did not come to the phone.

What is the Effect? after today, I may not be calling or sending anything for a while.

Character Trait Discussion
The Character Trait for Lesson Twenty-Three is "initiator".
An **initiator** is someone who begins something.

Read the statement below. Then choose <u>one</u> *of the questions below and answer it. Write your answer in the space provided then discuss it with your group.*

In this chapter, Grace is an initiator as she initiates a phone call to her mother on Mother's Day without being asked to do it.

1. Are you the one who initiates communication to your friends and loved ones? Explain how and when you do it.

2. Why is it important to be an initiator and not wait for someone to reach out to you first?

3. What would you do if you were in Grace's situation wherein you called to speak to someone and they didn't come to the phone?

_____Answers will vary from learner to learner._____

Lesson Twenty-Five - Answers

This lesson coincides with a diary entry dated June 16, 2019 from "Diary of Emotions: Thoughts and Feelings". The purpose of this lesson is to understand the author's feelings about her mother's reaction to the situation.
Entry Date: June 16, 2019

Main Idea and Supporting Details

Place an "X" on the line beside the "main idea" of the story.

__X__ Grace feels sad that her mother had not been coming to the phone.
_____ Grace is happy that she found her mother and knows where she is.
_____ Grace feels like the boarding home worker does not feel like getting Geneva to come to the phone.

The two statements below "support" the main idea. Fill in the blanks with the correct word.

(a) The boarding home worker told Grace that Geneva was in her **room**.
(b) Grace was not sure if it was Geneva's own **choice** to not come to the phone.

Interpreting and Evaluating Information

Write all the thoughts that could be going through Grace's mind about her mother in this entry.

Sample answer: Grace probably feels anxious and concerned about her mother since she is not talking to her. She tries calling her, but she never comes to the phone. Grace is feeling sad because her mother is again rejecting her in a way by avoiding talking to her. She might be guessing that it is over the money getting lost in the mail. Adding to the suspense, the working at the boarding home is not helping Grace was going and getting her mother to come to the phone. So Grace might be feeling a mixture of worry, sadness and disappointment. However, she is happy that she found her and knows where she is.

(However, answers will vary from learner to learner.)

Character Trait Discussion

The Character Trait for Lesson Twenty-Five is "complaisant".

Complaisant means willing to please others or to accept what they say or do without protest.

Read the statement below. Then choose one of the questions below and answer it. Write your answer in the space provided then discuss it with your group.

In this chapter, Grace is complaisant with her mother not coming to the phone despite her calling for the third time in a row to check on her. She finally accepts it and is just grateful for having found her.

1. Would you be complaisant with someone who does not want to talk to you? How?

2. Would you still be complaisant if someone was mean to you? State your reasons.

3. Do you think it is better to be complaisant to others, even if things don't go your way?

_____**Answers will vary from learner to learner.**_____

Lesson Twenty-Six - Answers

This lesson coincides with a diary entry dated August 6, 2019 from "Diary of Emotions: Thoughts and Feelings". The purpose of this lesson is to observe the author's change in attitude towards her mother.
Entry Date: August 6, 2019

Main Idea and Supporting Details
Place an "X" on the line beside the "main idea" of the story.

_____ Grace feels sad about Geneva making excuses to get off the phone.

__X__ Grace is wondering if she should continue to call her mother.

_____ Grace did not need to speak to Geneva when she called this time.

The <u>four</u> statements below "support" the main idea. Fill in the blanks with the correct word.
(Page 250)

(a) Grace is undecided about whether or not she should continue to **initiate** communication with her mother.

(b) Grace had sent her mother a **care** package and called to check if it had arrived.

(c) Grace told the worker that she did not need to speak to her mother, but just wanted to **confirm** if she had received it.

(d) The truth about her mother making excuses to get off the phone was **hurtful** for Grace.

Textual Evidence
From this entry, can you tell if Grace is putting some distance between herself and her mother? Pick two lines from the text to show this.

> "I called to let her know the package should have arrived, and spoke to her only briefly."

> When I called this time, I told the boarding home worker I do not need to speak to her. I just wanted to confirm she received the package.

Character Trait Discussion

The Character Trait for Lesson Twenty-Six is "respectfulness".

Respectfulness in this case, refers to having a courteous regard for people's feelings and wishes.

Read the statement below. Then choose <u>one</u> of the questions below and answer it. Write your answer in the space provided then discuss it with your group.

Being respectful of Geneva's wish to not come to the phone, Grace asks the boarding home worker to check if she had received the care package.

1. How would you know if someone wants to be left alone?

2. Why is it important to be respectful to others?

3. Would being respectful help to earn you respect? Why or why not?

_____**Answers will vary from learner to learner.**_____

Lesson Twenty-Seven - Answers

This lesson coincides with a diary entry dated September 15, 2019 from "Diary of Emotions: Thoughts and Feelings". The purpose of this lesson is to analyze the author's mother and identify the motive behind her actions.
Entry Date: September 15, 2019

Main Idea and Supporting Details
Place an "X" on the line beside the "main idea" of the story.

_____ Grace feels grateful to have found her mother and knowing where she is.

__X__ Grace feels it would be best if she discontinues phoning her mother.

_____ Geneva does not really enjoy being on the phone.

The four statements below "support" the main idea. Fill in the blanks with the correct word.

(Page 251)

(a) Grace does not feel like she should **call** her mother anymore.

(b) She will continue to call her mother only on **special occasions**.

(c) Geneva has been on her own for many years and Grace feels that she is **happy**.

(d) Geneva likes receiving gifts and mostly **money**.

Analyzing Character
What are the four things that Grace has understood about her mother from her actions?

1. **Geneva appreciates the interest that Grace and her brothers have in her.**
2. **She likes receiving gifts and mostly money.**
3. **She prefers to be to herself.**
4. **She probably feels more content without the phone calls.**

Making Inferences and Drawing Conclusions
Based on the entry, which statement about Geneva is most likely true?

(a) Geneva does not really want her family.

(b) Geneva prefers to be alone, even though she enjoys receiving things.

(c) Geneva does not care about hearing from Grace about her life.

(d) Geneva only cares about money and gifts.

Character Trait Discussion

The Character Trait for Lesson Twenty-Seven is "appreciative".
Appreciative means feeling or showing gratitude or pleasure.

Read the statement below. Then choose <u>one</u> of the questions below and answer it. Write your answer in the space provided then discuss it with your group.

Geneva is appreciative of Grace and her siblings caring for her even though she prefers to be alone.

1. Mention three things you are appreciative about right now, and explain why.

2. Do you think it is important to be appreciative of everything you have? Why or why not?

3. Have you ever been unappreciative of something until it went away? Explain.

_____**Answers will vary from learner to learner.**_____

Lesson Twenty-Eight - Answers

This lesson coincides with a diary entry dated September 22, 2019 from "Diary of Emoticns: Thoughts and Feelings". The purpose of this lesson is to understand the author's reason for discontinuing doing something.
Entry Date: September 22, 2019

Main Idea and Supporting Details
Place an "X" on the line beside the "main idea" of the story.

    __X__ Grace feels uncomfortable calling her mother.
    _____ Grace sent her mother a small package just to acknowledge her.
    _____ Grace really wants to know f Geneva had received the package.

The three statements below "support" the main idea. Fill in the blanks with the correct word.
(Page 252)

(a) Grace feels that Geneva is **content** without her calling.

(b) Grace has to **contend** with Geneva acting like she needs to get off the phone.

(c) Sending more packages would lead to Geneva carrying more items in her **backpack**.

Making Inferences and Drawing Conclusions
Based on the entry, why is Grace most likely to stop calling and sending things to Geneva?

Circle the letter of all the statements that could be true.

(a) Grace feels that Geneva is far away and that makes it inconvenient.

(b) Geneva does not come to the phone when she calls.

(c) Although Geneva likes receiving things, Grace finds it challenging.

(d) Grace wants to treat Geneva the way she treats her.

(e) There is a risk of the package getting lost in the mail.

Identifying Cause and Effect

"If she stores it in her bedroom, it will be stolen.
Therefore, I have every reason to stop calling and to stop sending things."

What is the Cause? If she stores it in her bedroom, it will be stolen.

What is the Effect? I have every reason to stop calling and to stop sending things.

Character Trait Discussion
The Character Trait for Lesson Twenty-Eight is "considerate".
Considerate means careful not to inconvenience or harm others.

Read the statement below. Then choose <u>one</u> of the questions below and answer it. Write your answer in the space provided then discuss it with your group.

Grace is considerate of Geneva and does not want to keep sending packages because she will have to keep carrying more things around.

1. Are you a considerate person? Mention some considerate things you have done.

2. Imagine you are planning to hold a party at your house with loud music, and there is a quiet elderly couple living next door. Would you still have the loud music?

3. Why is it important to be considerate to others and not always have your way?

_____**Answers will vary from learner to learner.**_____

_____

_____

_____

_____

Lesson Twenty-Nine - Answers

This lesson coincides with a diary entry dated September 24, 2019 from "Diary of Emotions: Thoughts and Feelings". The purpose of this lesson is to understand the author's decision to stop doing something.
Entry Date: September 24, 2019

Main Idea and Supporting Details

Place an "X" on the line beside the "main idea" of the story

    _____ When Grace called her mother, she actually came to the phone.
    _____ The worker at the boarding home did not allow Geneva to speak for long.
    __**X**__ **Grace has decided not to send her mother any more packages.**

The <u>three</u> *statements below "support" the main idea. Fill in the blanks with the correct word.* (Page 253)

(a) Grace called Geneva to let her know that the <u>**small**</u> package she sent should have been delivered to her by now.

(b) Geneva informed Grace that the last package she sent her was stolen by her <u>**roommate**</u>.

(c) Grace knew the type of <u>**environment**</u> that Geneva lived in and still sent the package.

(d) This had become the <u>**deciding**</u> factor for Grace to not send Geneva any more packages.

Reading for Information

Scan the text and find answers for the following questions.

(a) How much time did the boarding home worker give
    Geneva for using the phone?   **<u>Two minutes</u>**

(b) Did Grace spend a long time talking to Geneva on the phone?   Yes / **No**

(c) How did Grace feel when she overheard the boarding home
    worker speaking to Geneva?   **<u>confused</u>**

Analyzing Dialogue

Analyzing the dialogue or conversation between characters is important as it helps to better understand the plot of the story.

Conversation
She began asking questions about how my day was going and what I had been doing. I answered, then, in turn, I asked her how she had been doing. She sounded like she was really enjoying me and that she was happy I called.

What does this conversation reveal about Grace's mother, Geneva?

Answer: Geneva might have genuinely felt happy that Grace called her since it had been a while. She could have also asked her how her day was going in order to make her feel comfortable.

Identifying Cause and Effect

She said, "My roommate stole it!"
I said, "That is horrible!" I saw it as a care package gone down the drain, but I could not blame anybody but myself.

What is the Cause? She said, "My roommate stole it!"

What is the Effect? I saw it as a care package gone down the drain,

Character Trait Discussion

The Character Trait for Lesson Twenty-Nine is "supportive".
Supportive means being helpful and providing encouragement.

Read the statement below. Then choose <u>one</u> of the questions below and answer it. Write your answer in the space provided then discuss it with your group.

Despite the situation with her mother, Grace is still supportive of her and does things in her best interest.

1. Who is the most supportive person in your life? Explain why.
2. Would you still be supportive of a close family member even if they do not offer you the same support?
3. Should you be supportive of your loved one even if they do something wrong? Why or why

not?

_____**Answers will vary from learner to learner.**_____

Lesson Thirty - Answers

This lesson coincides with a diary entry titled "In Closing" from "Diary of Emotions: Thoughts and Feelings". The purpose of this lesson is to understand the author's thoughts on reuniting with her mother.
Entry: In Closing

Main Idea and Supporting Details
Place an "X" on the line beside the "main idea" of the story.

_____ Grace has decided to stop calling Geneva to confirm if she received packages.

__**X**__ **Grace explains the many challenges faced by families after reunions.**

_____ Grace has decided to let her mother call her instead.

The three *statements below "support" the main idea. Fill in the blanks with the correct word.* (Page 255)

(a) Grace says that people **assume** that all family reunions end happily ever after.

(b) Witnesses never find out what **really** happened after the reunion.

(c) The **emotions**, **thoughts** and **feelings** that Grace has experienced is nothing compared to finding her mother.

Reading for Information
Scan the text and find answers for the following questions.

What did Grace decide to send her mother instead of packages, and when?

Answer: <u>Grace decided to send her mother a small card with a very, very small amount of cash inside. She would send the card only on special occasions. She decided to do this because she need not risk packages getting lost in the mail and not get calls from Geneva.</u>

Character Decisions and Action

What caused Grace to change her attitude in regard to communicating with her mother?

(a) It was challenging to call and send her things because she is far away.

(b) Whenever Grace sends her mother a package, there is a risk of it getting lost.

(c) Geneva never calls to confirm that she has received the package.

(e) All of the above.

Interpreting and Evaluating Information

How does Grace feel about her reunion with her mother? Does she regret it?

Sample Answer: <u>Grace does not regret the reunion with her mother since she had been wanting to meet her for almost fifty years. She however describes the reality of family reunions that outsiders do not see. She says that there are challenges, questions and toiling after the reunion. She had experienced any emotions, thoughts and feelings with her mother after finding her. However, none of those things matter as finding her mother is the most important thing.</u>

Character Trait Discussion
The Character Trait for Lesson Thirty is "charitable".
Charitable means relating to the assistance of those in need.

Read the statement below. Then choose <u>one</u> of the questions below and answer it. Write your answer in the space provided then discuss it with your group.

Grace has always been charitable to her mother by sending her things even if she didn't ask for them.

1. Describe a time when you gave something to someone who was in need?
2. Do you think being charitable is better than being a receiver? Why or why not?
3. Do you think being charitable is a weakness or a strength? Explain.

Answers will vary from learner to learner.

ABOUT THE AUTHOR

Dr. Grace LaJoy Henderson is the author of over thirty books. Her latest inspiration is the new Finding Mother Series of four books, in which Grace LaJoy shares her story of finding her mother who abandoned her after forty-nine years.

Her foster care story, *A Gifted Child in Foster Care: A Story of Resilience, Classroom Set* and her children's book series, *The Gracie Series*, are currently being used in public and charter schools. Pearson Higher Education published two chapters from her foster care story in a college textbook. Newspapers, radio and television have also featured her publications and her story.

She has earned a Doctorate in Christian Counseling, a Master's of Education in Guidance and Counseling, and a Master of Arts in Curriculum and Instruction. She has also earned a Bachelor's degree in Social Psychology.

Dr. Henderson managed a contract with the Missouri Children's Division, in which she provided court ordered mentoring for foster youth, supervised parent-child visits and parent education. She has served as psychology and college success instructor as well as academic coach. Outside of higher education, she is a keynote speaker, workshop leader and guest author at schools, libraries and other organizations.

Dr. Henderson is dedicated to educating and consulting with aspiring authors. She has conducted Young Author Workshops for secondary students.

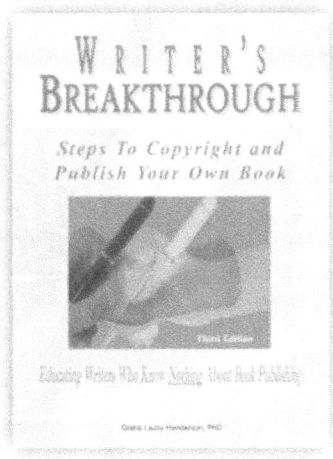

Writer's Breakthrough:
Steps to Copyright and Publish Your Own Book

Do you desire to publish your own book?

Do you have a book ready for publication but do not know where to begin?

Writer's Breakthrough will teach you where to begin, guide you step-by-step, and help you publish your own book. ISBN: 978-0-9829404-4-0

www.gracelajoy.com

FINDING MOTHER SERIES – SECONDARY / ADULT

A collection of nonfiction stories from Grace LaJoy's own life. This inspiring series reveals how the author was abandoned by her mother, lived in foster care, and reunited with her mother after five decades; and details about what happened after the reunion. *Questions inspiring mental health discussion and reading comprehension are included in the back of each book.*

When Grace LaJoy published her foster care story, **A Gifted Child in Foster Care: Story of Resilience**, she thought she would *never* find her mother. But, she found her after 49 years! Now, she is sharing her fascinating story in an *inspiring book series you will love!*

ISBN: 978-1-7341868-0-2

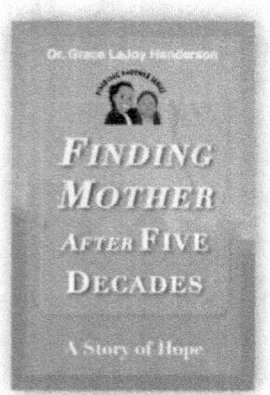

Mother After Five Decades: A Story of Hope
Grace LaJoy's determination pays off when she finds her mother who abandoned her at age two. Discover the details of her intriguing journey in *Finding Mother after Five Decades*.
ISBN: 978-1-7341868-3-3

Reuniting with Mother: A Story of Tenacity
What happens when Grace LaJoy and her siblings come face-to-face with their estranged mother after 49 years? How does she receive them? Find out in *Reuniting with Mother*.
ISBN: 978-1-7341868-4-0

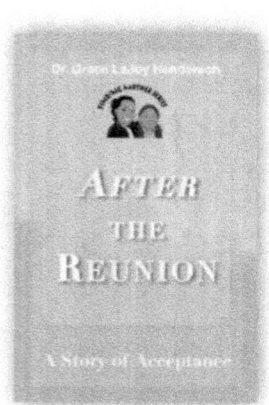

After the Reunion: A Story of Acceptance
After a very emotional reunion, Grace LaJoy has two concerns to address with her long-lost mother. What are her concerns? Does she get the answers she needs from her mother? Find out in *After the Reunion*. ISBN: 978-1-7341868-5-7

Diary of Emotions: Thoughts and Feelings
After reuniting with her mother after 49 years, Grace LaJoy toils with an array of thoughts and feelings. She reveals them all in *Diary of Emotions*. ISBN: 978-1-7341868-6-4

www.gracelajoy.com

A GIFTED CHILD IN FOSTER CARE – CLASSROOM SET

20 BOOKS, 20 STUDENT WORKBOOKS, 1 TEACHER'S GUIDE

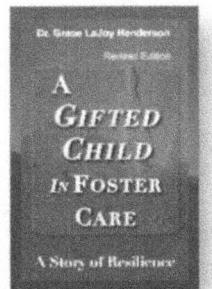

ISBN: 978-1-7341868-0-2

A Gifted Child in Foster Care: *A Story of Resilience*
In this book, Dr. Grace LaJoy shares her life story of being deserted by her mother, living in foster care, and ending up in a gifted and talented class while still in foster care. She recalls her life story before, during and after foster care. Her turbulent life experiences reveal how she became strong and began to encourage, inspire and empower others through her gift of writing. Finally, she offers words of inspiration, encouragement, and empowerment to both children and parents. Children learn that they can succeed and impact the lives of others even in the face of adversity. Parents learn specific steps to help children recognize and utilize their gift(s). 5.5x8.5 112 Pages

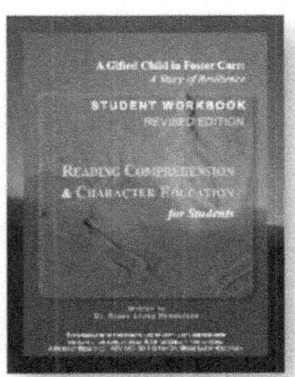

ISBN: 978-1-7341868-1-9

A Gifted Child in Foster Care: *Student Workbook*
Reading Comprehension and Character Education for Students. This workbook for students will assist teachers in fulfilling the state requirements of the Grade-Level Expectations (GLE's) for Language Arts. The lessons will improve reading comprehension for students, while changing attitudes and building character. Students will read the chapters in the nonfiction book, A Gifted Child in Foster Care: A Story of Resilience – Revised Edition, individually or as a group. Then they will do the lessons from the workbook that coincides with each chapter. Teachers will be able to lead students in critical thinking exercises. Students will be able to develop and apply skills and strategies to comprehend, analyze and evaluate nonfiction. 8.25x11 64 pages. Teacher's Guide sold separately.

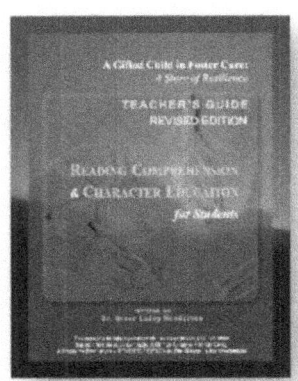

ISBN: 978-1-7341868-2-6

A Gifted Child in Foster Care: *Teacher's Guide*
Reading Comprehension and Character Education for Students. The Teacher's Guide contains the answers to the lesson activities in the Student Workbook, which is sold separately. It also contains additional lesson ideas that can be used in conjunction with the four core curriculum areas: Language Arts, Math, Science, Social Studies; also Career Preparatory and Communication Arts. In addition, it offers ideas about how to use "A Gifted Child in Foster Care" to teach more advanced reading comprehension skills. 8.25x11 68 pages.

Reading level grade 4+. Comprehension skills grades 4-7. Suggested for middle school students. However, high school students have been inspired by the author's story of resilience

www.gracelajoy.com

THE GRACIE SERIES – ELEMENTARY (READABILITY GRADES 2 – 3)

The Gracie Series follows the lovable character Gracie as she gets caught up in funny situations. Parents, teachers and librarians will enjoy sharing these engaging stories and listening as the children share their thoughts sparked by the discussion questions in the back of each book. Each story was inspired by entertaining memories from the author's own life, teaching valuable life lessons while inspiring young readers to use reason, analyze and think critically. Your child will love these heart-warming stories and so will you!

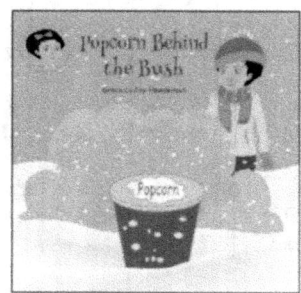

ISBN: 978-0-9987117-0-6 Soft
ISBN: 978-0-9987117-1-3 Hard

Popcorn Behind the Bush
A delightful little mystery about a tin of popcorn. When Grandma sends popcorn in the mail and Gracie does not receive it, Gracie goes on a hunt to find out if her family members can help her decipher a note left by the Mailman. Gracie is just about to give up hope when she finally solves the mystery!

Cake in My Shoe
A very determined little girl. Gracie makes a promise to her father, but comes up with a plan to break it when she sees her brother doing something she wants to do.

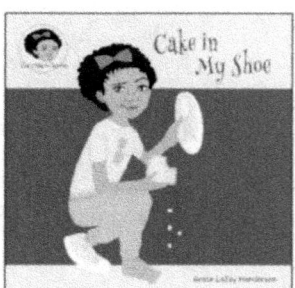

ISBN: 978-0-9987117-2-0 Soft
ISBN: 978-0-9987117-7-5 Hard

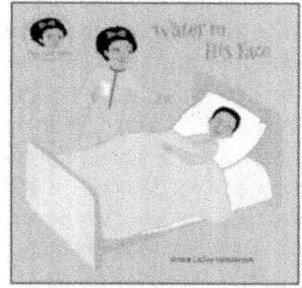

ISBN: 978-0-9987117-6-8 Soft
ISBN: 978-0-692-89977-9 Hard

Water in His Face
Gracie loves challenges! When Mother asks Gracie to help wake up Brother, she "jumps" at the challenge. But when her initial efforts to wake him does not work, she finally comes up with one last idea.

I Trimmed My Edges!
Grandma is coming over! When Gracie sees her family members making themselves look nice for Grandma, she wants to look nice for Grandma, too! What she does causes her family members to become outraged. But Grandma responds in a way that only a Grandma would.

ISBN: 978-0-9987117-5-1 Soft
ISBN: 978-0-692-89959-5 Hard

Math on the Table
Two children excited about math, but only one math worksheet. When Gracie finds a mysterious math worksheet on the table, she goes on a quest to find out how it got there. When she is not able to find out who it belongs to, she makes a decision that causes her to learn a valuable lesson.

Puppy Ate My Shorts
A naughty little puppy takes a bite out of Gracie's new shorts two times. But after hearing wise words from Father, Gracie makes a different decision the third time around.

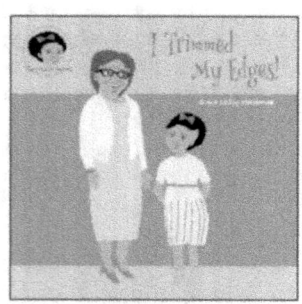

ISBN: 978-0-9987117-4-4 Soft
ISBN: 978-0-9987117-9-9 Hard

ISBN: 978-0-9987117-3-7 Soft
ISBN: 978-0-9987117-8-2 Hard

www.gracelajoy.com

MORE BOOKS BY DR. GRACE LAJOY HENDERSON

SECONDARY AND ADULTS

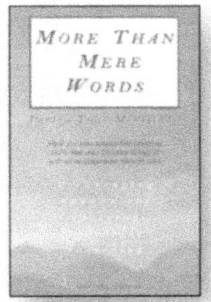

More Than Mere Words: *Poetry That Ministers*
Have you ever wished that someone could feel your Christian struggles and not be judgmental towards you? Have you ever needed just the right word at just the right time? Endorsed by Les Brown - author and motivational speaker, More Than Mere Words is a collection of powerful, spirit-filled, on-time messages. ISBN: 978-0-9747583-0-5

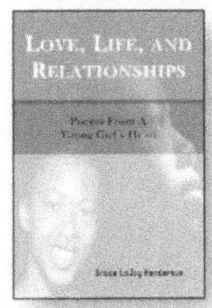

Love, Life and Relationships:
Poems from a Young Girl's Heart
Love, Life, and Relationships are poems written by Dr. Grace LaJoy, as a young girl, during the 1980's. The poems reveal her poetic thoughts about Love, Life, Friendship, Feelings, Hurt, Pain, Disappointment, Loneliness, Marriage, and Hope. ISBN: 978-0-9829404-8-8

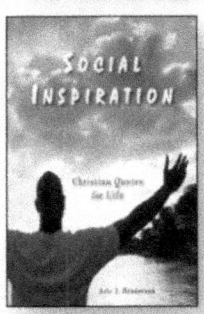

Social Inspiration:
Christian Quotes for Life is a compilation of quotes written by Dr. Grace LaJoy's son, Aric J. Henderson during his four years in college. These quotes are a combination of Aric's creativity coupled with Godly wisdom and even a little humor. ISBN: 978-0-9829404-1-9

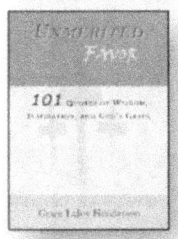

Unmerited Favor:
101 Quotes of Wisdom, Inspiration and God's Grace
A book of inspiring quotes written by Grace LaJoy Henderson.
ISBN: 978-0-9829404-6-4

www.gracelajoy.com

"Grace LaJoy Henderson's *Finding Mother Series* is a revelation. It is a gift to discover an author who can write so honestly—and with such vulnerability—about the joy and pain of reuniting with a parent after a 49-year separation. Henderson never glosses over the frightening or disappointing parts of her story. But her compassionate, unwavering voice, as she uncovers the long arc of her mother's life, is itself a triumph."
~Whitney Terrell, Associate Professor of English, University of Missouri-Kansas City

"The *Finding Mother Series* is a beautiful sequence of books. The author's reunion with her mother is very well documented."
~Phyllis Harris, Former Missouri State Director
Parent Information Resource Center

"The *Finding Mother Series* will inspire readers to *feel* their feelings. It stirs people in similar situations to be at peace, but at the same time seek growth, in the midst of their circumstances." Arica Miller, LMSW, School Social Worker

"The *Finding Mother Series* is a complex, touching opportunity for readers to see into the author's journey to find her mother after decades of searching. This series would be ideal for students at a secondary level who are searching for insight about the emotional conflicts and battles one must face when someone they care about has a mental illness. The four books in the series are segmented to provide specific lenses to the overall process, with a number of opportunities available for opening discussions about mental illness from both the author's point of view and her mother's." ~Leslie Arambula, M.A. in Creative Writing, English Teacher

"The *Finding Mother Series* displays a perfect example of how one triggering event can cause conflicting emotions. Throughout the series, the author experienced hope *and* despair, excitement *and* apprehension. Two, totally opposite emotions both at the same time. However, both were completely justified! This range and transition of emotions is what drives the entire series. Secondary students will absolutely benefit from reading this collection of books." ~Jacob Kelow, M.S.Ed., Secondary School Counselor, Kansas City Public Schools

"The author's emotional honesty and the balancing of positive and negative emotions is what makes this series work." ~Phoebe Shanahan, M.A. in English Literature

"The *Finding Mother Series* is written in a very powerful, real and authentic voice style. The author's honesty shines through her writing. Although the author's sadness throughout the story is quite palpable, her attitude towards her mentally ill mother is full of grace and understanding despite the fact that she had abandoned her. This is a clear and honest work."
~Fay Collins, Writer-Editor

Reducing stigma. Fostering connection. Inspiring hope.

www.ingramcontent.com/pod-product-compliance
Lightning Source LLC
Chambersburg PA
CBHW081228080526
44587CB00022B/3863